Praise for *Digital Homi*

When the pandemic hit, preachers were forced online with little time for reflection on what we were doing. Yang now offers us a theological introduction to the "digitalized Word" and explores ten (yes, ten!) different modes of proclamation offered to online viewers. Even after congregations returned to in-person worship, online worship and preaching have become a consistent part of most of our ministries. Yang leads the way with this conversation about best online homiletical practices in a world in which no one size fits all.

—Rev. Dr. O. Wesley Allen Jr., Lois Craddock Perkins
Professor of Homiletics, Perkins School of Theology,
Southern Methodist University

Sunggu Yang's *Digital Homiletics* is timely, theologically grounded, and helpfully practical. Readers will be pleasantly surprised by the usefulness of this book. For those who are delivering their sermons both in person and online, this book affirms their groundbreaking ministry and provides insights into how it can be done faithfully. It is a handy resource for any preacher who strives for effective preaching in the context of the digital age!

—Rev. Dr. HyeRan Kim-Cragg, principal and Timothy
Easton Memorial Church Professor of Preaching,
Emmanuel College in the University of Toronto

In the rapidly developing field of digitally mediated preaching, scholars tend to take either a theological or an empirical approach. In this book, however, Dr. Yang brings the normative voice of theology and the formal voice of homiletical theory into a dynamic conversation with the lived theology that is embodied in practices. The result is a much-needed, rich, in-depth discussion that considers both theology and the plurality of digital media. A must-read for any scholar or preacher who wants to understand digitally mediated preaching today.

—Rev. Dr. Frida Mannerfelt, author of *Co-preaching: The Practice of Preaching in Digital Culture and Spaces*

Preaching in digital space presents a host of crucial questions for those of us who want to preach with integrity and fidelity to our faith traditions. In *Digital Homiletics*, Sunggu Yang offers the friendly voice and trustworthy map so many of us desperately need. By addressing theological and practical dynamics, he helps us navigate this new and ever-shifting terrain with confidence.

—Dr. Donyelle C. McCray, associate professor of homiletics, Yale Divinity School

Whether you are a new or a seasoned preacher, a techie or a technophobe, Sunggu Yang's primer on digital preaching is for you. In an era of rapidly changing media and congregational disposition, preachers will find in *Digital Homiletics* practical expressions of what online preaching is and does—and, more importantly, a theological framework for considering what it might mean.

—Rev. Dr. Aimee Moiso, associate director, Louisville Institute; former managing editor of *Homiletic*

In *Digital Homiletics* Sunggu Yang extends his legacy of incisive theological inquiry to equip preachers for real-world challenges prompted by recent technological and ecclesiological developments. Beyond gimmicks or a bag of tricks, Yang drives us toward a techno-theological rationale strong enough to bolster imagination and resilience in preaching online. This is mandatory reading for all concerned with not just the what, the where, and the how of online preaching, but also the why and the who manifesting from digital pulpits.

—Rev. Dr. Jacob D. Myers, Wade P. Huie Jr. Associate Professor of Homiletics, Columbia Theological Seminary

This is the book the preaching community needs both now and in the future. Sunggu Yang continues to demonstrate that he understands the path that the Spirit is leading the church on. His concept of "the Word digitalized" is nothing short of groundbreaking and will become the ground on which future conversations about preaching and homiletics stand. Yang clearly loves the practice of preaching and those who engage in it. This volume, with its heavy focus on practical application, will well serve preachers who are discerning what preaching on the digital frontier looks, sounds, and feels like.

—Rev. Dr. Rob O'Lynn, associate professor of preaching and ministry, director of graduate Bible programs, and dean of distance education, Kentucky Christian University; author of *Digital Jazz: Preaching, Media, and Technology*

With so many options available for digital preaching, it can be hard to choose an approach. Sunggu Yang not only outlines different styles with practical advice for bringing them to life; he also places them in firm theological footings. This book is a wise guide for anyone navigating digital preaching.

—Rev. Dr. Richard W. Voelz, associate professor of preaching and worship, Union Presbyterian Seminary; director, The Bridge for Early Career Preachers; and author of *Preaching to Teach: Inspire People to Think and Act*

DIGITAL HOMILETICS

DIGITAL HOMILETICS

The Theology and Practice of Online Preaching

SUNGGU A. YANG

Fortress Press
Minneapolis

DIGITAL HOMILETICS
The Theology and Practice of Online Preaching

Library of Congress Control Number: 2023040713 (print)

Cover design: Kristin Miller (series design by Emily Harris)

Print ISBN: 978-1-5064-9099-1
eBook ISBN: 978-1-5064-9100-4

CONTENTS

CONTENTS

ACKNOWLEDGMENTS

Collaboration always.

I am sincerely grateful to the many members of the Academy of Homiletics who have been my close colleagues and research collaborators on various levels throughout the years. A significant number of their publications are referenced critically in this volume. I would like to extend special thanks to two anonymous reviewers and the senior editor, Dawn Ottoni-Wilhelm, of the academy's journal, *Homiletic*. Their considerate feedback greatly enhanced the academic rigor, pastoral insight, and editorial accuracy of the early version of this volume (originally conceived as an article). Their invaluable contributions continue to play a pivotal role throughout the volume.

I would like to express my heartfelt appreciation to two of my *Societas Homiletica* colleagues, whom I unexpectedly and happily befriended during the conference's annual meeting in Budapest, Hungary, in 2022: Frida Mannerfelt (Sweden) and Tone S. Kaufman (Norway). Their ongoing research in the field of digital homiletics and their kind encouragement regarding my own research have served as a distinct catalyst in maintaining my focus. Their words, almost literally saying, "Sunggu, we genuinely look forward to seeing your work published soon!" have provided invaluable motivation.

Valuable feedback was received from an assembly of international homileticians who convened at the University of Tübingen for a workshop in the summer of 2022. This feedback proved immensely beneficial when a segment of this volume was presented for their evaluation. I endeavored to integrate their multifaceted insights stemming from a variety of global viewpoints into various aspects of this undertaking. I am profoundly appreciative of their generous involvement with my work.

I cannot sufficiently convey my gratitude to all the creative preachers and congregations who explored a wide range of innovative methods of online preaching during the pandemic. It is their collective efforts that have made this volume possible. St. Andrew's Presbyterian Church in Oregon was one of these, inviting me to deliver a sermon on a Sunday morning during the pandemic via the church's Zoom platform. This experience became a cornerstone for developing the key content of Chapter 8 of this volume. Their invitation included an intriguing line: "You don't have to come to the church on Sunday morning. Please deliver your sermon from wherever you want. We will be everywhere as well." The liturgical world we encountered and continue to shape is truly remarkable!

Likewise, Korean Bethel Presbyterian Church also invited me to deliver an online sermon during the pandemic, an experience that formed the basis for Chapter 2—the Podium Style. Interestingly, they requested my presence at the church on Saturday evening for the recording of the entire worship service. All participants adhered to mask-wearing and social distancing protocols, and the recorded service was subsequently broadcasted on the following Sunday morning. This entire experience remains indelibly etched in my memory. For further details, please refer to Chapter 2.

ACKNOWLEDGMENTS

I wish to express my recognition to the Department of Practical and Missional Theology at the University of the Free State in South Africa for honoring me as a research fellow at an international level. Their unexpected invitation was a delightful surprise and has provided a distinctive boost to my academic pursuits.

Lastly, I extend my appreciation to the entire community of George Fox University, where I am presently engaged in teaching, and to my family, who have consistently been my most encouraging supporters in all my endeavors. Their unwavering backing is undoubtedly instrumental in my accomplishments and has shaped me into the person I am today. As I conclude this segment of writing, I want to reiterate my eternal gratitude to them.

PREFACE

Please read the preface.

Yes, I would encourage readers of this volume to read the following before proceeding to the main chapters. The concept of online preaching or the digital pulpit requires an a priori understanding to better explore its practicality and avoid confusion.

First, in this volume, I define online preaching as a digital live-stream form of preaching performed with no face-to-face congregation in front of preachers, even when preachers deliver their message in the church. Thus, online preaching is mainly for online listeners, or *sermon viewers*. We may think that online preaching is not really new. Similar practices like televangelism or live broadcasting of worship have been in practice for several decades. However, a big difference between online preaching and practices like televangelism or live broadcasting is that the latter is typically performed by "celebrity" or preachers of midsize churches in the presence of their congregations in physical church buildings; they broadcast their sermons with extensive technological support. Nowadays, however, any local preacher can practice online preaching to an online-only audience with minimal technological settings that nevertheless provide relatively high-quality live streaming.

Throughout the volume, pronouns for preachers were chosen carefully, with the intention of inclusivity, as there are preachers who use he, she, or they for pronouns. When referring to sermon listeners, as mentioned above in passing, I will most likely call them *sermon viewers* or *participant viewers*. Sermon viewers not only hear the sermon but *see* the preacher and the liturgical environment around the preacher through the digital screen. Surely, people sitting in the brick-and-mortar church pews and hearing the sermon "see" their preacher and the liturgical setting. Yet when it comes to online preaching, people's viewing is more intense and intentional (they must look into the screen to be part of worship!), a practice I call *purposeful viewing*. Besides, as we shall see, in many styles of online preaching, sermon viewers can actively participate in the sermon's meaning-making and delivery. Thus comes the designation of *participant viewer*.

Chapter 1 offers a homiletic-theoretic discourse on online preaching, while Chapters 2 through 11 present ten distinct styles of online preaching. Readers may wish to skip straight to Chapters 2–11 which explore practical, hands-on strategies and tips for online preaching. Reading Chapter 1, however, is encouraged as it provides a firm, unique theological and homiletical grounding for the practice of online preaching. Before erecting various columns, the walls, and the roof of a house, one must first lay the groundwork. A building can stand steady and strong only with firm foundations, as the time-proven wisdom goes. The same applies to online preaching. Sections titled "Select Adoption of the Seven Traits" in Chapters 2–11 may be less clear to those who have not read Chapter 1.

Chapters 2–11 consist of five main parts: general description of each different style of online preaching, details of the style, useful homiletic theory, practical tips, and final remarks. Most parts are self-explanatory, but the details of the style need some orientation here to get a firm grasp. Details of the style convey five distinct portions, as follows:

- *Who (Preacher's Role and Expectations)*: Comments on the unique identity construction of each different style of online preaching
- *Why (Merits: Homiletic, Spiritual, Ecclesial, etc.)*: Introduction of each preaching style's strongest advantages and its particular ecclesial context, as well as people's needs for this style
- *Where (Worship Space)*: Discussion of various places where each preaching style can or should happen
- *When (Time of Preaching)*: Consideration of when online preaching can happen given its flexibility or particular demands for live streaming or prerecorded broadcasting
- *What (Message Design)*: Proposal for general configuration of the sermon content, rather than specific instructions on what to write

What is suggested in Practical Tips is by no means exhaustive. Readers may want to expand on what's listed with regard to their unique context and practice. Other Resources, which provide two supplemental items for each style and are found at the end of each chapter, are helpful for that purpose. Please know that the ten styles, though exclusively discussed in the online preaching setting, are also applicable with slight modifications to in-person preaching. The ten styles may provide some food for thought for those considering different ways of creative and innovative preaching.

Online worship or liturgical matters—the immediate surrounding of online preaching—are rarely discussed, though here and there, they will be mentioned in passing. This volume solely focuses on the practice of online preaching. Several publications are already available in the market regarding online worship. Most of them are very useful, and I'd encourage the readers of this volume to refer to them as essential supplementals.[1]

Finally, the immediate context of writing this volume was the 2020-2022 global pandemic, when online preaching became a norm—a critical and vital part of the church's worship life. Thus, some references to this seismic event will be made here and there. Homiletical issues from that context will be discussed in several places, including the volume's introduction. Thankfully, the social and ecclesial impact of the pandemic has been fading away. The practical, homiletical ramifications of it, however, including online preaching, will stay with us for the foreseeable—or perhaps even unforeseeable—future, a situation which calls for the publication of this volume.

For that reason, I am very grateful to the staff of Fortress Press and especially my editors, Beth Gaede and Laura Gifford, who recognized that urgent call of the era and shared with me the vision for this volume. I could embark on this writing journey and finish only with their encouragement and support. I'm very much indebted to them, far beyond this short acknowledgment.

Notes

1 Among great resources available in this regard, readers may find the following open-access online journal issue invaluable: "Eucharist and Online Worship: Toward Extended Theological Reflection," *Currents in Theology and Mission* 50:1 (2023), available at https://currentsjournal. org/index.php/currents/issue/view/73.

CHAPTER 1

Context and Theology of Online Preaching

1.1 Context as Introduction[1]

Living through the time of the Covid-19 pandemic, online preaching has become a new norm for the pulpit worldwide. This new norm has demanded a novel theological conception of preaching, and eventually a fresh homiletic, strategic consideration of online sermon design and delivery. That is, we need a firm theology of online preaching as we develop new ways of practicing our preaching. The rationale is simple. Online preaching is different from conventional preaching, especially as practiced by mainline Christians. As we shall see in detail below, online preaching has its own techno-theological reasoning and unique ways of social communication. Without a critical comprehension of these, the practice of online preaching finds itself standing on shaky theoretical ground with no concrete performative strategy. Truth be told, this actually happened. When the pandemic hit the United States and other parts of the world in early 2020, most churches, not to mention preachers, were not ready for the novelty of online preaching. Even worse, there was not enough time to develop theological questioning and necessary homiletical resources. All that the preacher could do was "just do it online," which has generated many stories of unfortunate results. To be sure, some preachers have experienced hidden potentials in online preaching and presented stories of their innovations. But for many, a concrete theology of online preaching, as well as applicable homiletic strategies, were greatly needed.

The purpose of this volume is twofold: to provide a theology of online preaching and homiletical exploration of various styles of online preaching already in practice by early innovators. For that purpose, I begin with Karl Barth's threefold definition of God's Word to show one conventional theological understanding of preaching, and then proceed to scout a fourth emerging digital dimension of God's Word and its theological and homiletical implications. Barth is a personal, yet strategic, choice for a homiletic dialogue, thanks to the author's Reformed background and Barth's homiletical significance in that tradition. Yet, I hope that preachers and homileticians from other traditions may recognize common ground in his homiletical theology, and thus applicability of it to their practices of preaching. In this volume, whenever I use the descriptive word "conventional" (as in "conventional preaching"), it is intended to connote Reformed-conventional. Another notable limit of this volume, due to its primary concern with the practice of online preaching, is the lack of extensive consideration of online liturgical or worship contexts, though the latter is inseparable from the former and implied throughout. Focused consideration of online liturgy would be an important follow-up project to this volume.

1.2 Karl Barth's Threefold Definition of God's Word

Barth's threefold definition of God's Word provides one of the most compelling affirmations of the importance and practice of preaching that the preacher can carry in the Reformed liturgical context and beyond. For Barth, a prominent theological figure from the pre-online print culture,[2] the Word of God exists and presents itself in the following threefold form: the written Word of God (Scripture), the revealed Word of God (Christ), and the proclaimed Word of God (Preaching).[3] He explains that Scripture itself is not the Word of God until it is preached in the church's proclamation, and that we can know the revealed Word only from Scripture adopted by the church's preaching. Finally, preaching is only possible when it is rooted in the written Word and the revealed Word.[4] Accordingly, the three forms of God's Word never exist apart from each other, and without the other two, one form loses its fullest authenticity as God's Word. For Barth, this concrete unity of Scripture, Christ, and proclamation is analogous to the doctrine of the Trinity.[5]

What this threefold formula of God's Word generates in terms of theological and homiletical significance of each form of the Word is as follows. First, the written Word of God obtains the status of reliability and immutability or eternity. The written Word is reliable as it is the trustworthy source of the revealed Word and the preached Word flows from it. The written Word is immutable or eternal in the sense that no more written Word will be provided (that is, the canon is "set") and the canon will stay as it is for good, although other invaluable written words of faith will continue to emerge. Second, the revealed Word, as it represents the historical reality of the Word, generates two

3

of the Word's core characteristics, namely proximity and presence. Christ is always close to this world and ever present in the proclaimed Word. Third and finally, the preached Word, as it rises from the eternal Word and the historically revealed Word, is given an unmistakable authority due to its presumed tranformance (i.e., transformation of humankind, both individually and communally) and an assurance as the reliable Word of God. To summarize, Barth's idea of the threefold form of God's Word engenders these theological and homiletical traits of each Word:

- The Word of God written: immutability, reliability
- The Word of God incarnated: proximity (reality), presence
- The Word of God preached: transformance, assurance

Many homileticians across different cultural contexts, while embracing different theological foci, build their homiletic discourses and practices upon these traits of the Word (though not necessarily relying on Barth).[6] The Word is deemed reliable and eternal, always realistic and present in human history, and assuredly transformational. For them, therefore, preaching this six-trait Word is self-sufficient and enough for "success" for effective preaching in most, if not all, contexts. Anything more than these does not seem to be needed among those who, especially among Reformed traditions (including the Presbyterian homiletician and preacher Thomas G. Long), adopt some form of this "perfect" Trinitarian formula of the Word and its six eminent traits.[7] When the pandemic suddenly hit, however, it shook the theological ground of our homiletic theology and practices. A new fourth dimension of the Word has arisen, and it has great significance: *the Word digitalized.* A seismic change and challenge have followed with its rise, including the swift emergence of online preaching.

1.3 The Fourth Techno-Dimension of the Word: The Threefold Word *Digitalized*

It is presumptuous to state that the crisis of the Covid-19 pandemic alone spawned the fourth dimension of the Word—the Word digitalized and online preaching. The Word has been digitalized, and many around the nation practiced online preaching years before the pandemic. Yet the pandemic has contributed to the digitalized Word's vital and superior role in the ministry of the church as a whole, and particularly in the practice of preaching. For instance, online preaching is no longer a secondary option for worship but has become a primary method of sharing sermons with others.

A little more clarification on the definition of the Word digitalized may help here. Like the threefold nature of God's Word in Barth's formula, the Word digitalized is also threefold in its nature. In a nutshell, the Word digitalized includes the written Word, the revealed Word, and the preached Word; *all three digitalized.* Each Word deserves a more detailed description.

A. The Written Word Digitalized
The written Word *digitalized* means, first and foremost, the *paper Bible digitalized* and made available for free online.[8] This simple fact has had numerous digital and interpretive ramifications in recent history. To begin, the free online Bible has resulted in the common person's ability to readily compare different translations

of the Bible. Further, with some basic or even no knowledge of biblical Hebrew and Greek, people can now delve into the ancient meanings of biblical passages thanks to the availability of interlinear Bibles. Also, with various free online commentaries associated with online Bibles, people's interpretive skills and imagination can be enhanced without formal theological education. In addition, free resources of ancient noncanonical writings (e.g., the Gospel of Mary) broaden, if not challenge, one's view of the biblical horizon. Finally, for smartphone users, the Bible can be always near at hand as a theological and spiritual resource when raising and answering questions.

All these phenomena significantly challenge the two core traits of the written Word as previously discussed: immutability and reliability. It is not that mutability of the Bible arises as if one may now alter—add or delete—the given content of the Bible. Nor does it mean that the Bible is no longer reliable as a canonical authority. Rather, the interpretive and hermeneutical horizon of the written Word is wide-open: de facto, "beyond horizon." Any novel meaning of the written Word can be mined and applied to one's life, for good or ill. One's pursuit of the written Word's meanings is now boundless. Thus, the former traits of immutability and reliability give way to other traits of *fluidity* and *usability*. While immutability and reliability remain, fluidity of biblical interpretation or meanings and usability of the biblical content take priority over the former two and are much more important in most people's minds.

B. The Revealed Word Digitalized

The revealed Word *digitalized* denotes *Christ's image digitalized*, and more importantly, we can now encounter and enjoy a wide variety of digital images of Christ coming from different situations and cultures. A fine example is found in the painting of South African artist Maxwell Lawton, titled *Man of Sorrows*.[9] In the painting, Jesus appears not as a typical mighty or pastoral blue-eyed Caucasian figure but as a patient with AIDS who is in severe agony. The painting's message was not the suffering of AIDS itself but Christ's empathetic "healing touch" over AIDS patients as depicted by Lawton. Another example comes from Chinese Christian artist He Qi.[10] Qi effectively wipes away the western image and tone in his biblical paintings around the life of Jesus. Instead, Jesus and his followers appear as Asians with Asian apparel and other cultural expressions. The paintings bring the life of Jesus home to the very core of Asian psychology by representing Jesus no longer as a foreign stranger (who happens to be the savior for Asians from the west) but as an Asian ancestor who walked among Asians and whose whole life is given to Asians and others. Similarly, Korean Jesus portraits painted by Ki-Chang Kim generate a similar intercultural impact.[11]

One more unmistakable example is the digitally recreated face of Jesus published in 2002 in the magazine of *Popular Mechanics*.[12] A British team of forensic anthropologists in collaboration with Israeli archaeologists "re-created what they believe is the most accurate image of the most famous face in human history."[13] What they present to the world as "the most accurate image" of Jesus is the darker-skinned man of swarthy Middle Eastern ethnicity. As Alison Galloway, a professor of anthropology at the University of California in Santa Cruz, puts it, this digital image of Jesus is "probably a lot closer to the truth than the work of many great [Western] masters."[14]

What all these digitalized images of Jesus imply is the weight of intercultural omnipresence or cross-cultural ubiquity of the revealed Word in the world. This newly recovered trait of the

Word adds powerful specificity to the two conventional traits of proximity and presence of the revealed Word. The digitalized Word is not simply proximal to the world in an abstract sense or in a mono-cultural sense (e.g., the predominant white western image of Jesus) but enables each different culture to see and adopt Jesus as its own in a very meaningful way. Thus, it is now better to state that Jesus is *in and of* each wonderful culture than that the mono-cultural Jesus is present in different cultures.

Besides the newly added trait of cross-cultural ubiquity, the revealed Word *digitalized* is embedded with connectivity. This connectivity is possible thanks to 1) the images themselves connected by hyperlinks and 2) people's responses and reactions to the images now connected online. For instance, when a reader of this volume clicks digital links found in footnotes 9 through 12, the reader will instantly be directed or connected to the original sources of Jesus's images. If those sources have their own embedded links, the reader can move on to another set of sources. The pattern may continue nearly indefinitely. Through all these links and people's responses and interactions with one another, readers may encounter both amateur or professional comments.

In short, with the dawn of the revealed Word digitalized, the traits of proximity and presence absorb, if not give way to, whole new meanings of *ubiquity* and *connectivity* of the Word. These new traits generate easier and more familiar accessibility to the Word and many more—almost endless—possibilities for expressing the Word in fresh ways.

C. The Preached Word Digitalized

More than anything else, the preached Word *digitalized* indicates preaching that is performed for or through online spaces. Unlike the written Word and the revealed Word digitalized, however, the preached Word digitalized is, in most cases, accompanied and accomplished by the human body and voice, just like conventional in-church preaching. Yet the distinctive feature remains the same in that the preached Word digitalized (i.e., online preaching) is accomplished through *digital spaces.* In other words, between the online preacher and the online listener, there is a digital medium through which alone communication is possible. This factor truly distinguishes the preached Word *digitalized* from conventional ways of preaching.

Two critical interlocking questions arise from this: Does this medium or space help or hinder the listener's hearing? And if it is helping (or hindering), how can we use this medium most effectively? Given that most churches in the US today are using online spaces as one of their prime ecclesial communicative tools (e.g., worship broadcasting in hybrid services), it is desirable and fruitful to discuss its effectiveness and how to use online preaching wisely. To do so, we must further understand what digital space represents.

Principally and plainly, digital space is what is displayed on the screen of a digital device (e.g., laptops, desktops, TV screens, tablets, smartphones). Initially—that is, before the online revolution—this space existed mainly for the purpose of unilateral information transfer. For instance, a person could send a digitalized message or information through a hard disk memory device to another person who would receive and play it on the digital screen. Then the receiver might send back their information to the one who initiated contact in a similar way. Obviously, there was always a significant delay in communication between the two parties. In the late twentieth century, online digital space revolutionized this delayed transaction. Information now flows instantly between two parties back and forth.

(Think of Facebook Messenger.) Further, information can now flow between more than two parties, even thousands or tens of thousands of parties, in less than a second. Thus, a true bilateral and even multilateral communication via digitalized screens has been achieved.

As we live through the twenty-first century, digital space is not only used for information transfer but also for social transaction or *social interaction*. In addition to various types of social network services (SNS), like Instagram or Twitter, digital space provides nearly unlimited forms of social interaction. Two good examples are college education and worship services through Zoom. Students today enjoy live discussions with their peers on Zoom, while many churches live stream their services through this medium. Again, what is remarkable about this digital social transaction is its ability for *multilateral spontaneous communication*; numerous people from many different places and time zones can participate in communication at the same time.[15] In addition, online communication and interaction is instantly shareable with anyone around the world. In today's digital online industry, most successful companies design their products and contents in ways that allow them to be easily shared and distributed around the nation or the world with only one click or touch. *Spontaneity, accessibility,* and *shareability* greatly matter in the digital space.

Last but not least, one of the most critical dimensions of digital space is its highly artistic, holistic nature in communication. The digital space is artistic or aesthetically malleable as it takes advantage of a limitless number of calligraphic fonts, colorful images, object or human movements, various geometrical or mathematical figures, cartoon drawings, filmed natural scenes, photos, videos, music, lines, graphs, emoticons, and so forth.[16] This space is also holistic as it uses at least three of the five human senses: seeing, hearing, and touching (including screen touch and typing). The digital space can even be said to employ the other two senses of tasting and smelling as the clear and real-life images on the screen provide the brain with indirect experiences of the two remaining senses. In fact, when online bread and cup communion is practiced today, these two senses partake in the digital spiritual interaction.[17] In these ways, the availability of real-time video speaking in the digital space may be said to promote the space's holistic artistry.

When the preached Word is delivered in an online space, the Word digitalized is exposing itself to these new digital online traits: multilateral instant communication, holistic artistry, and shareability. In effect, these three new traits enable the preached Word's traditional traits of transformance and assurance to be possible in the digital space. When these new traits are absent or when they are not conscientiously developed, online preaching has a slim chance of wielding its spiritual magic of transformance and assurance. People simply would not get it if the Word preached in digital spaces did not adopt the new space's core traits. Frankly, the sudden onset of the pandemic did not allow enough time for preachers to adopt these new required traits of the digitalized Word, which in many cases has led to the ineffectiveness of the online pulpit.

1.4 Toward Effective Online Preaching

Six previous traits of the threefold Word are still strongly evident in the online pulpit because the preached Word still rises from the study of the written Word in the Spirit of the revealed Word. Yet, the new seven traits of the threefold Word *now digitalized*

11

have emerged as homiletic communicative essentials of online preaching to such an extent that it might be perceived as more significant than the former six. As discussed below, however, this should not be the case. Rather, the latter have added novel theological meanings and communicative characteristics to the former. In fact, the difficulties of online preaching mainly stem from unfortunate clashes between the previous six and new seven traits when preachers fail to integrate them.

The Threefold Word	Reformed/Conventional Preaching Traits	Online Preaching Traits
The Word, Written	Immutability, reliability	Fluidity, usability
The Word, Revealed	Proximity (reality), presence	Cross-cultural ubiquity, connectivity
The Word, Preached	Transformance, assurance	Instant communication, holistic artistry, shareability

The most challenging conflict is between immutability with reliability and fluidity with usability. The conventional authority of preaching rooted in immutability and reliability of the Word no longer remain as the highest considerations. Rather, wide-open fluidity and pragmatic usability of the Word are crucial for people's engagement with preaching and thus preaching's communicative effectiveness. In other words, fluidity and usability have become hugely important contributing factors for preaching's authority and reliability.

The second most notable clash occurs between assurance and instant communication with shareability. In online spaces, the preached Word digitalized is itself a form of digital information, and this information travels very quickly, in less than a second. The margin to measure the assurance of the preached Word becomes very narrow. However, there is no reason to utterly despair. People's sharing activity of the preached Word itself (e.g., the global spreading of the good news preached from a local preacher) helps obtain a digital form of assurance. Simply put, the fact that people can and do share the preached Word widely, instantly, and voluntarily is a positive sign that the Word's assurance is being retained.

The above two examples of apparent clashes between the conventional six traits and the emerging seven traits of the Word are not nearly as consequential as their potential for compatibility and collaboration. The previous six are in great need of self-transformation, while the emerging seven heavily rely on the six for mutual enhancement. In this sense, effective online preaching would be wise to combine the "old" six traits with the new seven traits in a new configuration of homiletical theory and practice. Certainly, this is tough work for any preacher today: it requires a lot of critical reasoning and strategizing, as well as better digital infrastructures in local churches. Yet it is undeniable that this tough work is demanded of the church as well as society. Preachers are called to walk along this challenging digital road. We must respond to needs and requests from the "digital pews" (that is, anywhere and everywhere people now worship online) as pastorally as possible.

As we will see in the following chapters, all the seven traits of the Word *digitalized* can be naturally or intentionally embedded in all ten styles of online preaching. Also, there is homiletical overlap among the ten in terms of the utilization of the seven traits; that is, different styles share several traits. Note that each style is best developed when maximizing a select set of traits.

Finally, this categorization of the ten styles can help preachers be aware of various strategies that are available for adaptation when faced with many different online contexts and audiences.

Chapters 2–11 will showcase the ten styles of online preaching, some being more popular and widely practiced than others. Yet, all ten styles have recently garnered wide attention and are gradually being employed by more and more preachers; for this reason, it is important to know more about them all. Admittedly, there could be and have been (and will be!) more than ten styles of online preaching. These ten are not chosen because they are deemed to generate the most effective forms of homiletical communication but because they are the most widely available and reliable options at this point for the preached Word digitalized. Now, it's time to explore each of them. Welcome aboard.

Notes

1 The original version of Chapter 1 and some parts of Chapters 2–11 appeared in the journal of *Homiletic* 46. no. 1 (2021): 75–90. This volume presents a modified and much updated content.

2 In a sense, Barth is a beneficiary of his own era's technoculture—namely print culture, along with the emerging radio, TV, and film industries of his time, as Walter Ong would argue. (See below.) This statement seems quite right when we consider the church's heavy reliance on print—one of the most advanced technologies of the Reformation era with its dual purposes of knowledge dissemination and spiritual formation. Barth obviously took great advantage of print technology for similar purposes in generating multiple publications, including the little book, *Homiletics*. This implies at least three things. Pre-online print culture should not be considered an era of no technological advancement (that is, we should not have a condescending posture toward print culture; truth be told, we still

heavily rely on print for social discourse). Second, Christian knowledge dissemination and formation is still bound to a great extent to print culture in the current era of digital revolution, although print's historical significance is gradually diminishing. This volume by no means implies that print culture has no relevance in today's world but only that the digital revolution is swiftly taking over the role of print culture and therefore necessitates novel ways of knowledge production and personal formation. Third, Barth's homiletical argument based on print culture (e.g., the written Bible) presents its own limitations as the Bible itself has a strong oral/aural history. Yet, Barth upheld the Bible as the most reliable source for God's revelation due in part to the unavailability of the oral tradition which preceded and contributed to it. (Karl Barth, *Homiletics* (Louisville, KY: Westminster/John Knox Press, 1991), 75–80.) Walter Ong, a major literary critique and cultural historian of the twentieth century, recognizes "writing" as "a technology." With the dawn of writing technology, he contends "hearing-dominance" has yielded to "sight-dominance." From this perspective, it would not be wrong to state that online digital preaching further promotes, if not maximizes, sight-dominance as people now *watch* (and listen to) preaching through the digital screen, rather than being mere listeners of the sermon in the conventional homiletic-communicational model. More will be discussed later regarding this matter. (Walter J. Ong, *Orality and Literacy: The Technologizing of the Word* (New York: Routledge, 2013), 80–81, 115–120.)

3 In Barth's own words, the Trinity is "only one analogy to this doctrine of the [threefold] Word of God." (Karl Barth, *Church Dogmatics: The Doctrine of the Word of God, Volume I, Part 1*, ed. G. W. Bromiley and T. F. Torrance, trans. G. W. Bromiley (New York: T&T Clark, 2004), 110.)

4 Barth, *Church Dogmatics The Doctrine of the Word of God, Volume 1, Part 1*, 120–21.

5 Barth, *Church Dogmatics The Doctrine of the Word of God, Volume 1, Part 1*.

6 Homileticians may not give equal emphasis to all six traits, but rather employ a more nuanced focus on one or two of the six, depending on the specific homiletical topics or contexts considered, while still having all six in mind. For instance, Lucy A. Rose focuses on dialogical proximity and presence of the incarnated Word in her roundtable homiletic proposal, Justo L. González and Pablo A. Jiménez on postcolonial transformance and assurance of the preached Word, and Luke A. Powery on the written Word's reliability in terms of its pneumatologic nature of lament and celebration. See Lucy Atkinson Rose, *Sharing the Word: Preaching in the Roundtable Church* (Louisville, KY: Westminster John Knox Press, 1997); Justo L. González and Pablo A. Jiménez, *Púlpito: An Introduction to Hispanic Preaching* (Nashville, TN: Abingdon Press, 2005); Luke A. Powery, *Spirit Speech: Lament and Celebration in Preaching* (Nashville, TN: Abingdon Press, 2009).

7 Long acknowledges biblical preaching as "the normative form of Christian preaching." For him, the Bible is the precious and most authoritative conveyor of God's revelation recorded and cherished by the faith community throughout history. The written Bible, Long continues, is eminently Christ-centered (meaning that we are encountered by Christ in it), assuring of Christian faith, spirit-transformative, reliable for life's guidance, and counter-imaginative vis-à-vis "the consumerist, militaristic, death-obsessed imagination of the culture." For Long, preaching must, therefore, arise from this unique and canonical Christological document. It seems that, in other words, Long believes in and affirms confidently the six traits of conventional Barthian preaching as the core nature of biblical preaching. Thomas G. Long, *The Witness of Preaching* (Louisville, KY: Westminster John Knox Press, 2016), 59, 60–62.

8 For more articulation of the term digital or digitalized, see C. The Preached Word *Digitalized* section, below.

9 The image is available in one of his interviewed articles found in Joriel Foltz, "VCU Without Borders," *Shafer Court Connections*,

spring 2006, 9. The image is also available on YouTube: AP Archive (@APArchive), "South Africa: Jesus Aids Painting," YouTube video, July 21, 2015, https://www.youtube.com/watch?v=pmMxQC6k4xo.

10 Many of his Asian images of Christ, along with portraits of other biblical stories, are available at HeQiArt.com: "Welcome to He Qi's New Gallery," Welcome to He Qi's New Gallery, accessed October 10, 2020, https://www.heqiart.com.

11 Several images are available on a Korean newspaper webpage, http://m.daejonilbo.com/mnews.asp?pk_no=1090321. For more scholarly discussions of the Asianness of Jesus, see Rasiah S. Sugirtharajah, ed., *Asian Faces of Jesus* (London: SCM Press, 2013), esp., chapter 5, "Jesus Christ in Popular Piety in the Philippines," by Salvador T. Martinez.

12 Mike Fillon, "The Real Face of Jesus," *Popular Mechanics*, April 10 2020: Mike Fillon, "The Real Face of Jesus," *Popular Mechanics*, 2023, accessed October 10, 2020, https://www.popularmechanics.com/culture/a41336100/real-jesus-face..

13 Fillon, "The Real Face of Jesus."

14 Fillon, "The Real Face of Jesus."

15 On social media, as Stine Lomborg and Charles Ess point out, the user (the listener in the case of online preaching) "is now increasingly the producer or author of much of the content posted in these venues." Stine Lomborg and Charles Ess, "Keeping the Line Open and Warm": An Activist Danish Church and Its Presence on Facebook," in *Digital Religion, Social Media, and Culture*, Pauline Hope Cheong, *Digital Religion, Social Media and Culture: Perspectives, Practices and Futures* (New York: Peter Lang, 2012), 169. As will be discussed later with reference to the Zoom/Chat-style of preaching, online listeners can now actively contribute to the final content of the sermon as the authentic "producer" or "author" of the sermon.

16 See Robert S. Fortner, *Communication, Media, and Identity: A Christian of Communication* (Lanham, MD: Rowman & Littlefield, 2007), especially. chapter 6, "Communication as Art." Fortner provides a

comprehensive articulation of how and why (digital) communication is art or artistic (having aesthetic dimensions).

17 For online communion, people typically prepare their own elements at home and consume them when the pastor or priest blesses all the elements at different places, including in the pastor's or priest's church where the online worship and preaching occurs during live streaming.

CHAPTER 2

The Podium Style

Figure 1[1]

General Description

This is the most familiar, and likely most popular, online preaching style for most practitioners. Preaching is typically live streamed, or recorded for later viewing, from the pulpit of the brick-and-mortar church; thus, this style of online preaching is not really distinguishable from conventional pulpit preaching. However, a notable difference is the absence of a physical congregation in the church. Typically, all the pews are entirely empty. People are invisible to the preacher, present only in the digital space. They can see the preacher, but the preacher cannot see them. This may make the preacher uncomfortable.[2] The preacher should maintain eye contact with the camera throughout the sermon, even if they are using a less formal podium or moving around. Multiple cameras set at different angles can enhance the experience. While much of the practice of conventional pulpit preaching can remain the same, the dynamics of the preaching performance can be quite different and even challenging, given the preacher's focus on the camera. As a quick note, in the writing hereafter, I intentionally adopt the word podium over pulpit (or use them interchangeably), to be more conscious and inclusive of various types of modernized pulpits. These may look different from conventional ones, especially in the practice of online preaching.

Details of the Style

Who

This style will best serve conventional brick-and-mortar pulpit preachers, or preachers who prefer manuscript delivery of the sermon over spontaneous delivery. Often the Podium-style preacher will wear formal clothing, as the image shows above, and make more use of formal language. Along with their key verbal communication, various facial expressions and hand gestures would serve as supplements. As aforementioned, the preacher faces the challenge of having to have their eyes fixed on the camera most of the time—this practice creates an illusion for sermon viewers that the preacher is looking into their eyes at the moment—except when reading the manuscript.[3] Finally, despite the physical or movement constraints of the style the preacher can still be creative in the fine execution. For instance, as discussed in more detail in the "Practical Tips" section below, the preacher can make good use of visual and aural aids more freely than when they preach in a conventional in-person setting, and also, in the case of the recorded sermon, the preacher can benefit from sophisticated digital editing. The possibilities for creativity are practically limitless.

Why

As implied above, a high level of comfort and familiarity is the prime reason why preachers choose this style. The preacher can use the same worship space or environment with other familiar worship or liturgical furniture and elements around them, which they might have used for a long time. The only thing they do not have is the same people in front of their eyes, while all they newly need is a high-quality digital camera with live-streaming or recording capacity. Thus, not much liturgical or technological adjustment is needed, and the adjustment can be quick.

That is the second prime reason why this style was a choice by many during the Covid-19 pandemic from 2020–2022. Because of the unexpected, sudden arrival of the fatal virus, preachers needed to adjust their preaching quickly. They needed something doable right away; the Podium style rightly met their urgent need!

In an ecclesial sense, the same may apply to sermon viewers, especially conventional churchgoers who feel comfortable with a similar message delivery style. Though the sermon is now on the digital screen, there is no need to radically adjust their listening patterns or environment. All they need is a smart TV, tablet, laptop, or smartphone through which they can watch. Additionally—probably the most important liturgical or psychological merit—sermon viewers appreciate the familiar worship setting they are used to that is now being "brought" to their ordinary life spaces; in a sense, they are still worshipping "in the church."

Where

Above, we primarily talked about the conventional brick-and-mortar worship space as the chief venue for the Podium style, and admittedly, this is most convenient. However, this style can be adopted anywhere and everywhere, both physically and digitally. To begin with, physically, as long as the preacher has something to serve as podium furniture and a digital recording or live-streaming camera set, the preacher can easily practice the style in many different places: the preacher's church office, home office, the church's parking lot, or even in nature.

Thanks to satellite internet equipment, like Starlink or hot spot functionality, outdoor live streaming is easier than ever before. Admittedly, as discussed before, congregants may prefer their preacher to deliver a message from the familiar worship setting. However, from time to time, delivering a message from a place that can nourish the key points of the sermon may be welcome. For instance, when preaching Psalm 23, what about standing near a real flowing water with its dribbling sound and delivering a refreshing pastoral message?

If physical relocation sounds a bit extreme, digital relocation would be a highly plausible alternative. Digital relocation means creating an imaginative or realistic background for the worship space. Zoom users may be familiar with this technological trick. The preacher can still stay in the physical church building, but by overlaying the digital background, the preacher can now be "anywhere and everywhere." As a quick example, when preaching on Acts 2, preachers may want to put themselves in the middle of the Upper Room, digitally and imaginatively recreated. Or when preaching about Matthew 3, preachers may want to "relocate" to the Jordan River where Jesus is baptized, with the river's background image surrounding them. Practically speaking, there are no limits to the implementation of digital relocation in accordance with the church year or the specific message that the pastor preaches.

When

Typically, preachers prefer or would choose live streaming, as most preaching viewers expect them to deliver the message live on Sunday morning or at other scheduled times. When live streaming, the maneuvering of the streaming camera is very important, especially if, as is typical in most churches, a church happens to utilize only one fixed-angle camera with some basic movements possible, like left and right or zoom in and out.

As many other liturgical elements happen along with the sermon, it is crucial that the camera technician conduct a rehearsal with the preacher and other worship leaders to make sure of the right angles of the camera in each movement. When prerecording the sermon on other days and times of the week, the whole technical enterprise gets both easier and more complicated. The preacher or the technician may be able to do sophisticated editing on the recording, deleting unnecessary parts and "errors" in speaking or performance, which will help create a "clean shot" of the sermon and aforementioned digital relocation.

However, other worship leaders, who would not necessarily be present during the prerecording, must make sure that the prerecorded sermon aligns with other parts of the service. Churches may not be able to afford to bring in worship volunteers on weekdays, most of whom should be available on Sunday mornings. In sum, both Sunday morning live streaming or prerecording on other days is possible but should be determined by the context of the church and the preacher's capacity.

What

Among all the ten styles of online preaching explored in this volume, the Podium style may present the most recognizable formality in terms of message construction. Many preachers would write up the whole manuscript and read from it at the pulpit, with improvisation depending on each preacher's capacity and personality. Even those with good memorization or spontaneity ability tend to produce the complete manuscript and try to memorize as much as possible before the delivery.

It is not that the Podium style's message will always be strictly didactic, prosaic, and humorless. Rather, formality is a naturally shared ethos between the preacher and the sermon viewers due to the conventional symbolism of the podium ("one of the oldest pieces of furniture" in human history, as preacher Fred Craddock once noted). The preacher can still be humorous, poetic, or wildly imaginative, but there will be a good sense of formality throughout the message construction and delivery.

The Podium style's message is more straightforward, with clear topical points. People's attention span on the digital screen is very short, particularly when it comes to one-way formal, verbal communication. Clarity, coupled with short, memorable phrases and punchlines, will surely help the preacher's message get across the people's ears and digitized consciousness.

Useful Homiletic Theory

In the era of TikTok, Instagram Reels, and YouTube Shorts on which video clips run only for fifteen seconds to ten minutes (and mostly, less than one minute), it is difficult to keep people's attention focused on the screen for a fifteen-minute sermon. The Podium style may have more difficulties in keeping people's attention than the other nine styles discussed later as the podium has a general ethos of "lecturing." However, certain homiletical theories and strategies help mitigate this challenge. After all, people still listen to and watch longer clips on the screen that have solid content and well-strategized communication (think of thirty-to forty-minute-long podcasts and online education lectures). Two following theories may be good aids: Episodic Preaching and Four-Page Preaching.

In my work on preaching and the arts, I have introduced episodic preaching as a novel homiletical concept that can be highly effective for today's media-saturated sermon hearers.[4] This preaching concept has two essential interrelated homiletical characteristics. The first is its highly episodic-existential character. An episodic preaching sermon feels like a creative amalgamation of mutually relevant short sermonic episodes or episodic meaning blocks; in a well-managed, fully stretched case, each meaning block may stand alone as a complete sermonette, with no need of others. Thus, this method distinguishes itself from a typical narrative or essay mode of preaching as Introduction-Body-Conclusion. Instead, episodic preaching may flow as Meaning Block One, Meaning Block Two, Meaning Block Three, Meaning Block Four, and Meaning Block Five. The Introduction and Conclusion might be there, but not necessarily in a formal sense. Meaning Blocks One and Five would serve as Introduction and Conclusion. The highly existential quality of each block makes the whole episodic scheme possible.

A second characteristic is that, thanks to the existential quality of each move, the resolutive good news, aha moment, or key topic of the sermon can be found everywhere—that is, in each meaning Block. This somewhat confusing literary ploy makes better sense when compared to inductive and deductive moves of preaching. Admittedly with a certain degree of oversimplification, we can say that inductive preaching generates the climax or the most conclusive gospel message toward the end of the sermon, while deductive typically does the polar opposite. In either case, the gospel climax is set to appear at "fixed" places: at the end or at the beginning.

In episodic preaching, there are no fixed places. The gospel moment can happen in each and every meaning block, depending on each sermon's design. This does not mean that each block presents a separate sermon topic. All meaningful moments or topics will be relevant to each other. Nor does this imply that there will be no sermonic flow. An exemplary flow is possible with the following structure: Hook and Development; Climax (Confrontation and Resolution: The Gospel Existentialized); and Renaming, Implication, and Denouement: Reorientation of the Self. In sum, the existential-episodic quality of the sermon, which may create an illusion of hearing several different episodic messages in each short meaning block, and its possibility of the generation of various gospel moments through the entire literary flow, helps greatly to keep people focused on the sermon.

Briefly, the Four-Page Preaching method, based on Paul Scott Wilson's *The Four Pages of the Sermon*, is also helpful in maximizing the effectiveness of the Podium style. Again, any hearer's attention span on the digital screen is very short, and digital hearers tend to be more focused when something new *and* meaningful happens through short intervals. Four-Page Preaching is optimized for that, as each Page presents a different or new meaning block of the sermon: Page One (Problem in Scripture), Page Two (corresponding Problem in the World), Page Three (Solution or Gospel in Scripture), and Page Four (corresponding Solution in the World). "Page" is a metaphor for each sequential meaning block in the sermon. Thus, "page" can mean one paragraph, two, or three (but surely, less than four, as four will create a very long meaning block).

Being somewhat creative with Wilson's methodology in order to satisfy the short listening pattern of digital hearers, the preacher may want to create six or eight Pages by doubling or dividing the original Four; for instance, Page One (Problem 1 in Scripture), Page Two (corresponding Problem 1 in the World), Page Three (Solution 1 in Scripture), Page Four (corresponding Solution 1 the World), Page Five (Problem 2 in Scripture), Page Six (corresponding Problem 2 in the World), Page Seven (Solution 2 in Scripture), Page Eight (corresponding Solution 2 in the World). The sermon time and scriptural interpretation will decide how many Pages should be created.[5]

Whether using Episodic or Four-Page Preaching, what is at the stake is the optimal use of the Podium style. The Podium style will probably stay with us as it has for thousands of years as one of the most convenient and effective ways of religious communication. Doing away with it entirely in the digital era won't be an option. The question thus becomes how to make the best use of it.

Practical Tips

- **Select Adoption of the Seven Traits:** While all ten styles of online preaching can adopt the seven traits in unique ways, each style will show certain traits to their advantage more than others. For example, the Podium style can maximize the effect of the trait of **ubiquity**; in particular, Christological-spatial ubiquity. This Christological ubiquity happens when the preacher speaks from the conventional church's pulpit or platform, which carries with it a sense of sacredness, encouraging association with Christ's presence in the digital space. Metaphorically interpreted, the preacher's church space is connected (the trait of **connectivity**) with that of the listener, which "transforms" the latter's space into a sacred one as well. The holistic artistry of the Word might be lacking to some extent in this style since the camera angle is mostly fixed on the lecture style preacher, yet its strong trait of ubiquity conveys the possibility of inviting the symbolic feel of the church's artistic nature (e.g., the aesthetic pulpit area design) into the sermon viewer's digital screen space.

- **Optimize Use of Digital Editing:** Digital editing is possible in two major ways: spontaneous and/or planned. Spontaneous editing means digital editing occurring during the live streaming of preaching; examples can include the use of visual and aural aids appearing on the screen during the sermon (e.g., sound effects or photos), zooming in and out of the preacher's particular body motions (e.g., palms in the posture of receiving), the camera's focus on the communion bread, an instant summary of the preacher's message, and so on. Planned editing means digital editing of a prerecorded sermon. Planned editing may include all the editing maneuvers of spontaneous editing, but also can use additional tools. For instance, as a widely used editing tool for longer speeches, the sermon recording can be divided up into major meaning blocks and brief (a second or two) pauses can be inserted between them; the pause or interval can be filled with silence, sound, a summary text, or relevant image. This editing gives the sermon viewers freedom to watch one or two segments first, and then others later. They may even move around in the sermon freely for their own review or rewatch particular segments, knowing where to start and pause. This editing is great for today's people with short digital attention spans. Sermon viewers may enjoy watching each short segment of the sermon at their own pace.

- **Incorporate Punchlines:** Memorable short phrases or punchlines that generate musical rhythms of the sermon, create its episodic sense, and are repeated here and there throughout the sermon will help the preacher's message get across to people's easily distractible ears and digitized consciousness. In that sense, as a structural stretch, three-point preaching may work very well too. The rhythmic and clear structure may help the sermon hearers to easily follow along with keen attention. Of course, the preacher should make sure not to create three different minisermons within one sermon, but rather to create well-integrated three points within one sermon.

- **Try Verse-by-Verse:** This time-proven ancient method of preaching—Origen (185-253 CE) is known to use this method extensively—can be an effective one for the Podium style.[6] A real strength of this method is each verse's interpretation and its immediate hermeneutical connection with the congregational world.

This can help generate the feel of bilateral communicative interaction between the preacher and the sermon viewers, the lack of which is a well-known downside of Podium-style preaching.

• **Use a Teleprompter:** The teleprompter is a real gift if the Podium style online preacher happens to practice full manuscript sermons. While preaching (or reading through the manuscript), the preacher can look straight through the camera lens, keeping constant eye contact with the imagined audience. This is a huge factor in drawing people's continued interest and attention to preaching. A quick caution: the preacher should be aware that the teleprompter may hinder the preacher's spontaneous message-making or other creative moves, as the appliance somewhat tends to fix the preacher's focus on the written words appearing on the screen. Each preacher should be able to find their own innovative ways of using a teleprompter to resolve any communicative-performative issues. Many kinds of economical teleprompters that typically require a separate tablet computer for screen display are now available in the market.

Final Remarks

Podium-style preaching was the most popular—and most adopted—online preaching form used during the COVID pandemic across denominational and cultural boundaries. It was simply the most reliable, familiar, and economical in most local churches. A crucial challenge was how to make the style more digital environment-friendly, maximizing the great strengths of this style. Thankfully, preachers have shown their creative digital adaptability of the traditional brick-and-mortar pulpit. The same critical challenge will always stay with us: How can we make the style more user- and listener-friendly in an ever-changing digital environment? In that sense, the Podium style has a "happy" task of facing and resolving each different digital revolution's challenge. Podium-style preachers must feel excited!

Other Resources

Carrie La Ferle and O. Wesley Allen Jr., *Preaching and the Thirty-Second Commercial:*
Lessons from Advertising for the Pulpit (Louisville, KY: Westminster John Knox, 2021).
This source helps preachers formulate impactful messages, with punchlines or catchphrases, for today's sermon listeners whose aural and visual senses are heavily saturated with highly persuasive short marketing clips and messages.

Alyce M. McKenzie, *Making a Scene in the Pulpit: Vivid Preaching for Visual Listeners*
(Louisville, KY: Westminster John Knox, 2018).
As the title clearly indicates, this fine volume provides practical homiletical strategies for designing and delivering vivid scene-creating sermons. Sermon samples are very useful.

Notes

1 For example, see https://www.youtube.com/watch?v=E8s70HIvl0U &feature=youtu.be (accessed October 10, 2020).

2 In 2021, I had the privilege to deliver a Sunday morning message at a local Korean American church in Oregon. It was a Sunday message, but because of the pandemic constraints, the church prerecorded the

entire worship on Saturday evening. When I arrived minutes before the recording session in the sanctuary, the media and tech manager of the church made a cordial request to me: "Pastor, during the whole sermon delivery, please look only at (through) the center camera. Hundreds will be watching this service tomorrow, and we want to make sure that they know the preacher is speaking to them." At first, I thought that looking at the camera the entire time would be easy, but as soon as I got onto the podium and began the message, I realized this wouldn't feel as comfortable as I'd imagined. First off, there were still people—worship staff and other volunteers—in the pews, though very few, looking at and listening to me. Because of training and habit, I found myself looking at or preaching to them with my eye contact away from the camera, which I was conscious of throughout the whole delivery! Second, it felt simply unnatural and strange to try to talk through the camera for the whole thirty minutes or so, knowing that this was not even live streaming, thus nobody was actually watching it at the moment; in a sense, therefore, I was, indeed, preaching to nobody in the moment. I should say feeling unnatural before the camera is normal for most preachers.

3 In 2021, I had the privilege to deliver a Sunday morning message at a local Korean American church in Oregon. It was a Sunday message, but because of the pandemic constraints, the church prerecorded the entire worship on Saturday evening. When I arrived minutes before the recording session in the sanctuary, the media and tech manager of the church made a cordial request to me: "Pastor, during the whole sermon delivery, please look only at (through) the center camera. Hundreds will be watching this service tomorrow, and we want to make sure that they know the preacher is speaking to them." At first, I thought that looking at the camera the entire time would be easy, but as soon as I got onto the podium and began the message, I realized this wouldn't feel as comfortable as I'd imagined. First off, there were still people—worship staff and other volunteers—in the pews, though very few, looking at and listening to me. Because of training and habit, I found myself looking at or preaching to them with my

eye contact away from the camera, which I was conscious of throughout the whole delivery! Second, it felt simply unnatural and strange to try to talk through the camera for the whole thirty minutes or so, knowing that this was not even live streaming, thus nobody was actually watching it at the moment; in a sense, therefore, I was, indeed, preaching to nobody in the moment. I should say feeling unnatural before the camera is so normal for most preachers.

4 See chapter six, "Preaching to Episodic Ears (Drama)," from Yang: Sunggu Yang, *Arts and Preaching: An Aesthetic Homiletic for the Twenty-First Century* (Eugene, OR: Cascade Books, 2021), chap. 6.

5 Paul Scott Wilson, *The Four Pages of the Sermon: A Guide to Biblical Preaching* (Nashville, TN: Abingdon, 1999).

6 For a more detailed introduction of this method, see Allen: Ronald J. Allen, *Patterns of Preaching: A Sermon Sampler* (St. Louis, MO: Chalice Press, 1998), 29.

CHAPTER 3

The Conversation Style

Figure 2[1]

General Description

In this style, the preacher is a friendly conversation partner with "invisible" listeners or sermon viewers beyond the camera. The preacher typically sits behind a table, looking at the camera on the same optical plane/level. The background and the surrounding environment feel comfortable and friendly, perhaps including a plant or a vase of flowers in sight. Most importantly, the preacher's presence is pastoral, with a vocal tone and style of speaking that is conversational. With the preacher on the same visual plane as the camera, viewers feel like they are sitting across the table from the preacher. The preacher "converses" with individuals behind the camera lens, often offering rhetorical or actual interpretive questions to aid the viewers' perceived or imagined participation in the sermonic event. Rather than using

35

a manuscript, preaching with short notes often works better in this style as the preacher is expected to keep constant eye contact with the camera (that is, with the listeners).

Details of the Style

Who

This style is recommended for preachers who have adopted the Podium style as their mainstay and want to change the mode of sermon delivery, but not too radically. Compared to other styles explored in the following chapters, this style's creativity level is relatively manageable and cost-effective, and as in the Podium style, the preacher has significant control over the sermon content and sermon delivery; that is, a minimum level of spontaneity is required. For conventional brick-and-mortar pulpit preachers, this style is an easy try.

Secondly, for more people-oriented, relational preachers, this style could serve them best. They will be able to create, and even experience for themselves during sermon delivery, better relational-pastoral intimacy between the preacher and the listeners, which is rarely achievable in typical digital sermonic communication other than in the Zoom/chat style. (See Chapter Nine.)

Why

As implied above, the relational-pastoral intimacy between the preacher and the listeners is one of the strongest merits of this style. In certain contexts, like during the pandemic or when some listeners are temporarily or permanently disabled,[2] in-person contact between the preacher and listeners can hardly happen. Naturally, this degrades the relational intimacy between the preacher and the listeners. The Conversation style may become an effective aid in these kinds of unfortunate situations, increasing the impact of pastoral care upon listeners.

Another great merit of this style is an active, though limited, biblical-interpretive interaction between the preacher and the congregation. For instance, the preacher could solicit a certain number of questions or comments on the sermon passage from the listeners prior to the worship service, then incorporate them into the actual sermon delivery. This way, a preacher may elevate the level of the congregation's attention to, and their participation in, the sermon's meaning-making. See below in Practical Tips for more details.

Where

Unlike the Podium style, which typically happens in the physical church building setting, the Conversation style can be practiced in the church building, the preacher's office, or even at the preacher's residence if needed (like in cases when the church building is closed due to a pandemic or severe weather). In the case of the sample sermon (follow the link in footnote 1), which happened during the beginning of the COVID pandemic in 2020, the pastor set up a "pulpit table" in front of the actual pulpit area and recorded the sermon during the week to be broadcasted later. An interesting element is that the viewers of the sermon do not actually see the church's pulpit area thanks to the digital curtain—created by digital editing of the original recording—behind the sitting pastor, which may have created a very comfortable seeker-church type of ecclesial environment. Of course, preachers may want to show the whole pulpit area in an ecclesial setting where the congregation is accustomed to the traditional liturgical ethos. In either case, the preachers, since they will still be preaching from the pulpit area or the theater-type contemporary worship stage, may find themselves relaxed in a familiar preaching space.

Again, though, preaching from an office or home are also fine possibilities. Given close collaboration with the digital worship design team (if there is a team!), the preacher should be quickly able to cope with emergency occasions and turn her everyday familiar place into a sacred worship ground with a simple table and a digital curtain.

When

Both live streaming on Sunday morning or broadcasting after recording are possible depending on the pastor or the church's preference and circumstance. Obviously, when doing live streaming, it is crucial to collaborate with the worship design team or assistants, especially in the use of the worship space in the physical building. It will be important to move the pulpit table without the worship viewers noticing if it must be placed in the desired spot in the middle of a live service. To avoid any logistical issues either when preparing the service with a team or for themselves, preachers may want to record the sermon during a weekday and incorporate it into the rest of the live-streamed worship. In the latter case, it will be important for the beginning and ending of the message to fit well into the overall flow of the service.

What

As the style's name designation indicates, dialogical or conversational message construction works best for this style. This style's major difference from the Zoom/Chat style explored in Chapter Nine is its more intentional formality in message construction.

Clearly, this style will present less formality than that of the Podium style in terms of its amiable verbal tone and less reliance on fully scripted communication. Simple sermon notes (outline), or no notes at all, depending on the preacher's preference and capacity, will help maximize communicative effectiveness. The preacher is expected to "converse with" the sermon viewers through the camera lens. Of course, the preacher may still have a full manuscript—left behind at the study desk—from which to get a useful outline. Even when writing the full manuscript, the preacher will have the imaginative sermon dialogical partner in mind, wittingly creating enough room in the manuscript itself for that imaginative dialogue. For instance, during the conversational sermon delivery, novel questions may pop up in the preacher's head, which is typical in actual in-person dialogue. When that happens, rather than sticking to the (partially memorized) manuscript or the sermon notes, the preacher may develop a somewhat new direction in the sermon. In sum, modest room for spontaneity or impromptu communication works fine in this style.

Useful Homiletic Theory

Several homileticians have provided useful theoretical insights that are helpful for the Conversation style. Here is a quick summary:

Insight One: Rhetoric of Listening

In conversational preaching, we may conceive of preaching as a "rhetoric of listening."[3] First and foremost, before actual preaching, the preacher listens to interpretive insights (on a particular text) from the congregants, stories of their lives (in relation to the text), and previously silenced voices from the margins of the congregation (now empowered by the text). This art of listening can be achieved by a dialogical form of preaching that McClure names "collaborative preaching." Dialogical collaborative preaching here does not involve either holding conversations from the pulpit, nor a two- or three-party dialogue sermon in which two or three preachers speak for one sermon. Rather, his proposal is "to move closer to a model of single-party preaching that faithfully represents a collaborative process of sermon preparation."[4] When this collaborative process is successful, preaching may include "the actual language and dynamics of collaborative conversation on biblical texts, theology, and life,"[5] and it can empower congregational self-leadership and mission centered around Christian Scripture. This collaborative process can helpfully abate the predominant individualized or privatized faith construction of Christians in Western society today. In life, or even in worship, we tend to look for texts that address our individual lives only and apply lessons and insights of the text to our own situations. When people come to the interpretive roundtable together and share their (different) thoughts on the text with *others*, especially those from the margins of society or the congregation, people soon begin to expand their siloed hermeneutical horizons, which makes the interpretation and application of text richer and wider.

Insight Two: Complete Incompleteness

"Complete incompleteness" of the sermon is totally acceptable in the conversational style.[6] We preachers tend to want to have full control of the sermon's message, and even how the message is perceived by the listeners. For instance, when there is one key message in the sermon, the preacher wants to have that message transferred and "planted" in the minds of the listeners exactly in the way the message was constructed—thus, all listeners must have one single, same message at the end of hearing the sermon! Most preachers know that this is an ideal that is rarely achieved. What actually happens phenomenologically is that listeners will construct their own unique interpretive meanings of the same message. Surely, their interpretive meanings could be similar or even identical to each other at times, but only rarely. This phenomenon I call complete incompleteness. In the sense that the preacher's message is not delivered to or perceived by all the listeners as one single complete message, the sermon is incomplete. But still, that incompleteness of the sermon is *complete*, or at least good enough, if the preacher has communicated the message faithfully and sincerely. This complete incompleteness should be a, if not the, modus operandi of the conversational style of online preaching, as conversation by its nature is meant to be open-ended communication enabling conversationalists to create their own meanings out of what is communicated back and forth. Simply put, preachers, when speaking in the Conversation style, are encouraged to be more conscious about their tendency to exert full control over the sermon's message and be more intentional in allowing the listeners' own meaning-making of the sermon's message.

Insight Three: Roundtable Membership

Implement a rotation system for membership in a sermon roundtable. Allow the same group of individuals to participate for a designated period, such as three or six months. Afterward, consider forming new groups with volunteer participants from the congregation, including "invisible" members who may not have previously been involved. In that sense, inviting children or youth into the "adult" roundtable is a great possibility, thus creating an intergenerational group. Also, purposeful creation of a multicultural or multiracial group, as well as groups of different genders and sexual orientations, should be put into consideration. After all, ideally, listening to *the whole congregation* during a certain span of time is highly encouraged.

Practical Tips

- **Select Adoption of the Seven Traits (see Chapter One): Fluidity** and **usability** are the two hallmark traits in this style. As the preacher creates a conversation with listeners akin to the *Round Table Pulpit* model proposed by John S. McClure, the preached or conversed Word will welcome many different interpretations of Scripture. That is, the preacher's interpretation and application of Scripture in this style are generally wide-open as the preacher invites the listeners' own fluid explorations and applications of it in their unique *Sitz im Leben*. In this way, the listeners become virtual contributors to the preaching event.

- **Conversation over the Text:** Ideally, the preacher will initiate pre-sermon conversations on the preached sermon text at least about two weeks—and ideally, a month—before the sermon is delivered. As McClure suggests, the preacher and the congregation (the focus group or a random group each week) can do this through regular weekly in-person meetings. Recently, two other feasible options have become available: weekly Zoom roundtable talks or Google Docs brainstorming.

○ Zoom talks are desirable for congregations that favors live interaction among (un)familiar church members. A minor disadvantage of this method is that people may not become fully candid in expressing their opinions about the text in front of other participants.

○ With Google Docs, the facilitator-preacher may ask participants to write their own thoughts on the text and put their names (first or last name only, or initials), or perhaps not use any identity signifiers so that they feel much more comfortable. The preacher may want to open a new Google Docs file on a new text at least a month before actual preaching and encourage the congregation to become collaborative exegetes. As Google Docs allows for making comments on each other's written pieces, the preacher and the participants should be able to have rich written "conversations" along the way.

○ For more tech-savvy and smartphone-using MZ generations (millennials/Generation Z), Google Docs may feel "boring" and inconvenient. (In a practical sense, it's not convenient to open and type on a Doc via a smartphone.) For them, doing similar collaborative textual exploration on social media and chat platforms—like Twitter, WhatsApp, WeChat, KakaoTalk, or Facebook groups—is much more familiar and convenient.

Conversations can become more creative on those platforms (e.g., conversations involving various emoticons). Do a simple survey around the congregation regarding what method or digital platform most of the population prefers.

- **Directional Yet Open-Ended Questions:** Without a proper direction, exegetical conversations on a given text could develop in almost every imaginative way, which is not ideal for a single sermon. Thus, a certain direction is needed, albeit with a good degree of open-endedness; this preacher-provided direction should not become a hindrance to the participants' wide, healthy interpretive imagination on the text. Simple yet thought-provoking directional questions are ideal either at the beginning of the Zoom talk, Google Docs file, or other engagement. The following questions are only a handful of samples among endless possibilities (as surely, each different text would demand a different set of questions):

  ○ What connection do you see between this given text and what comes before and after the text?
  ○ What interpretations or ideas have you heard about the given text?
  ○ Whose voice is loud and whose voice is silenced in this parable?
  ○ If any, what images or personal memories come to mind when reading?
  ○ What objects in this story get your immediate attention?

- What words or phrases get your immediate attention?
- What conflict(s) do you see in this text or story?
- What does God seem to be doing in this text?
- What does this story seem to want the readers to learn and do upon hearing?
- Do you fully agree with what the author of the text seems to say and affirm?

- **Sermon Beginning with Questions:** Since good conversations can begin with good questions, it would be great to begin the conversational style sermon with a good question or a series of questions as an introduction to the sermon. What questions, then? The preacher may want to utilize the same or similar questions as are used for a particular text, as shown above. As the congregation (or a select group) has explored the text with the familiar questions over the past weeks or month, they would greatly appreciate the preacher's handling of the questions at the pulpit table. Naturally, those questions will draw the viewers' attention and help their active engagement with the sermon.
- **Several Questions, If Not a Question per Move:** Each move (i.e., a significant meaning block) of the main body of the sermon may begin with a thought-raising question. Again, this is the Conversation style, which means that the preacher should create an imaginative dialogue with the audience and keep the dialogical tone of speaking throughout the sermon. Good questions dropped along the full sermonic

movement help the preacher achieve both well! Of course, the whole sermon should not become like a long Q&A session on the text. The preacher will have a concrete message to proclaim, again with a certain degree of open-endedness. Questions are engineered to smoothly get to the message that is shareable in a friendly way with the dialogical sermon viewers.

- **Hand Gestures and Facial Expressions:** The preacher should know that as the preacher always stays seated, the viewer's immediate attention goes to the preacher's torso, hand gestures, and facial expressions. When emphasizing certain points of the sermon, use appropriate hand gestures as shown in the above sample image. Otherwise, it would be better to put both hands on the table softly and naturally so that the preacher appears well-poised. In the sample image, the preacher holds a mic; however, if possible, a lavalier microphone may work better as it gives more freedom to the preacher's hands. Too many dramatic facial expressions would not work well in the Conversational style. (Of course, they would work best for the Drama style discussed in Chapter Seven.) Before the delivery, preachers who opt for this style may want to do a mental exercise of imagining themselves naturally talking with a friend over coffee.

- **Simple Props and Background:** If needed, small simple props that could assist the sermon's points would work well. Again, those props should not generate too much dramatic impact. Changing the preacher's background image in accordance with the focal message of the day is possible and even at times recommended. The same can easily apply to all styles of online preaching discussed in this book.

Final Remarks

We now live in a time when people hunger for good conversations. Good conversations give us delight and help us mine hidden or forgotten meanings of life. Through this style the preacher can become a delightful conversation partner for the congregation, even through the screen—again, remember that some folks can be only approached through the screen for various reasons. Then, preaching must be a wonderful source of strength and grace for daily life and a catalyst for the robust *conversational* ecclesiological life.

Other Resources

Lucy A. Rose, *Sharing the Word: Preaching in the Roundtable Church* (Louisville, KY: Westminster John Knox, 1997).
This resource is good for preachers who wish to see differences—theological, homiletical, and practical—between conversational preaching and other conventional forms of preaching.
O. Wesley Allen Jr., *The Homiletic of All Believers: A Conversational Approach* (Louisville, KY: Westminster John Knox Press, 2005).
Allen proposes and develops a very helpful concept, namely "conversational ecclesiology," that is crucial in practicing conversational preaching. Chapter 5, "A Case Study based on the Revised Common Lectionary," provides useful samples of conversational preaching, including its lectionary-based homiletical logistics.

Notes

1 For a sample, see https://www.youtube.com/watch?v=psICh2IP2-E&feature=youtu.be (accessed March 1, 2022).

2 Shannon Dingle, "Quitting Online Church Is Abandoning the One for the 99," Religion News Service, accessed March 1, 2022, https://religionnews.com/2022/02/02/quitting-online-church-is-abandoning-the-one-for-the-99/. In her article, Dingle presents how much online church or preaching has helped the spiritual life of disabled people during the recent pandemic.

3 John S. McClure, *The Roundtable Pulpit: Where Leadership and Preaching Meet* (Nashville, TN: Abingdon, 1995), 7.

4 McClure, *The Roundtable Pulpit: Where Leadership and Preaching Meet*, 48.

5 McClure, *The Roundtable Pulpit: Where Leadership and Preaching Meet*, 8.

6 See chapter two, "Picasso and Preaching (Cubism)," from Yang, *Arts and Preaching: An Aesthetic Homiletic for the Twenty-First Century*, chap. 2.

CHAPTER 4

The Reporter Style

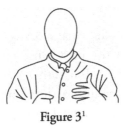

Figure 3[1]

General Description

For the Reporter style, the preacher stands without the pulpit and the conventional altar in the background and does not use a full manuscript.[2] Typically, the preacher will use a virtual background that can be made of photographs, moving images, or church images. All of this contributes to the creation of highly *situational preaching*. The key homiletical strategy is the production of the sacred event that seems to be happening *here and now* in the world, and right in the middle of worship, where the preacher "reports" from the vantage point the position gives. As a result, preaching in this style sounds like fact-based, "live" reporting. Usually, other digital-liturgical elements will accompany preaching (such as prayers, candle lighting, choir singing, etc.) before, during, or after the sermon, as well as real-life pictures or news photos, recorded music, live interviews, and relevant performances such as sacred dancing. Sophisticated technological support is essential in ensuring high-definition visual quality and smooth transitions between various liturgical elements.

Details of the Style

Who

In this style, the preacher plays the role of reporter of the sacred event. During the preaching, the preacher does not preach from the church, but rather the digital background transports the preacher into a shopping mall, a friendly or violent neighborhood, a shoe factory, a national museum, etc. Preachers who choose this style find themselves "actually" witnessing, describing, and making comments on the focal scene and other details happening *out in the world*. Yet, as a homiletical reporter, the preacher's reporting is hermeneutical reporting. In other words, the preacher wisely uses Christian Scripture as a critical interpretive lens in finding and naming God's grace in the people's mundane *Sitz im Leben*.[3] The preacher, then, literally and metaphorically, is a mediator between the world of Scripture and the world of the newspaper, to borrow Karl Barth's analogy. Yet, a reporter is a reporter. The preacher as the reporter does want to appear as one excessively overlaying or imposing the interpretation on what is observed; rather, the preacher should present as a reliable source for the sermon reviewers in their own pursuit of faith-enhancing facts, truths, and information. In that sense, preachers of this style often find themselves dancing around the two poles of interpretive subjectivity and informational objectivity.

Why

A prime ecclesial and spiritual merit of this style is the dissolution of the conventional sacred and secular dichotomy. In a more friendly terminology, this style can "bring the church" or worship space into the sermon viewers' daily lives. Preaching or worship now happening in people's daily life environments—what a wondrous union of the sacred and the secular through worshipful moments! Admittedly, this mind-blowing wonder is only a "feel" made possible by online technological maneuvering—that is, with preachers standing and making their reports in and from the digital or virtual reality world. Yet still, the preacher's virtual participation in people's real-life environments and issues can be very powerful in a pastoral sense. Virtual reality itself—films, YouTube clips, podcast talks, TV news media, online magazines, Zoom calls, daily emails, etc.—is already an essential part of real life. We could say that real life in the twenty-first century is only possible through virtual life, and vice versa. The preacher's virtual participation in people's real life can be beneficial as part of genuine congregational care. A second noticeable homiletical merit of the style is the potential of elevating the credibility of the preacher, if not preaching itself. As preaching is more incorporated with photographs, live events (recorded or live streamed), people's interview clips, and so forth, the sermon listeners would perceive of preaching as more facts-based and life-touching rather than as secretive ancient Scripture-based or jargon-filled theological talking. Thus, there should be, when the style is executed well, a better chance for them to develop in their mind more credibility of the preacher and what is proclaimed.

Where

Technically, the Reporter style is possible anywhere and everywhere beyond the church building. As long as the digital background technology, which is relatively painless, is available, this style can be adopted with ease. For effortless liturgical communication and collaboration with the whole worship crew, the preacher may stay in the church. It may, however, be ideal and meaningful to alternate the preacher's physical or virtual location between the church and other real-life settings, moving back and forth and creating the liturgical "magic" of the preacher taking the church to the streets and bringing the streets to the church. This will enhance the dynamic and bilateral dissolution of the sacred and secular dichotomy. As a fun tactic, when the sermon is based on a biblical story with several narrative characters, preachers may want to "transport" themselves into the ancient world with the help of the creative background. Then, they would be reporting imaginatively from the ancient world!

When

Both live streaming on Sunday morning or other worship days and prerecording are viable options. Live streaming will require a significant amount of rehearsal time with a reliable tech crew as most digital-liturgical elements should happen in perfect sync with preaching; photographs, moving images, music video clips, and different backgrounds should appear right on time. In that respect, prerecording can be easier. Preaching with no other digital-liturgical elements could be recorded on any day or time, and then all other elements added through studio editing. Yet, to allow ample time for editing, it would be wise for the preacher to record the sermon before Friday, if Sunday is the target broadcasting day, with the editing crew working on it for the rest of the week.

What

The sermon content of the Reporter style will most likely rise through contextual hermeneutics; in particular, the contemporary contextual approach to Scripture. In other words, the content will be the result of faithful and critical dialogue between the listeners' contemporary real-life circumstances, including that of the preacher and biblical texts. In actual delivery, the preacher formulates the contextual hermeneutical result into the reporter's message with phrases such as "I haven't seen..."; "This is what is happening now here..."; "People I have met said..."; "As you can see now on the screen..."; or "About this moral phenomenon, experts' explanation is..." Thus, in conjunction with the verbal message, the preacher may make good use of the digital screen by showing data graphs, photos, video clips, literary quotes, and so forth. These visual and/or aural aids aren't simple homiletical aids; rather, they themselves can be real messages almost equivalent to the preacher's verbal message. Remember St. Augustine's famous comment on the relation between sacraments and preaching: "The sacraments performed as the visible word, and the word proclaimed as the audible sacraments." In sum, in the Reporter style, there are two types of equally weighted messages proclaimed: verbal/aural and visual.

Useful Homiletic Theory

The Swedish homiletician Frida Mannerfelt sheds an important and helpful insight into the making and delivery of Reporter-style preaching, even though she does not have this specific homiletical style in mind.[4] She analyzes religious digital creatives (or RDCs) and their homiletical role. In a conventional understanding, RDCs, or digital technicians in a more friendly terminology, mostly work behind the scenes during online preaching—for instance, rolling cameras and editing sermon recordings—and are *not* considered figures of religious authority nor direct contributors of the sermon's message-making. Mannerfelt, through her literary and empirical research, turns the tables entirely. For her, RDCs *are* copreachers of online preaching and equally weighted contributors to sermon-making. Even religious authority is, or should be, evenly split between online preachers and RDCs. Mannerfelt found that the making of online sermon content and its delivery became truly whole and possible only with significant contributions from RDCs (of course, admittedly, limited to her own case studies, which are not universal). Thus, again, her conclusion is that RDCs *are* copreachers.

As delineated above, the Reporter style requires very close collaboration with digital technicians or RDCs. (We now have a new language.) RDCs may provide insights on scriptural interpretation, suggestions on camera shooting locations, decisions on the relevant image and music selection, critical judgments on sermon recording and editing, sermon feedback collection and analysis, and much more. As Mannerfelt notes, all these are essential parts of crucial hermeneutical reading of Scripture and practical-semantic maneuvering in the sermon's making, delivery, and evaluation. RDCs should then be seriously considered copreachers; the preacher is not a lone speaker but a polyphonic sermonic collaborator. All this seems like a true achievement of the ancient meaning of liturgy, namely, the people's collaborative work.

Thomas G. Long's perception of preaching as bearing witness and the preacher as witness is very helpful, as well, in articulating the preacher's teleological identity in the Reporter style, for reporters and witnesses share basic functions of event- or storytelling. According to Long, preaching as bearing witness means, among others, the following: 1) the preacher's authority rises from what the preacher has seen and heard in the text and the world, but not from any institutional religious commissioning, 2) the preacher as witness testifies to events which are all about the holy encounter between God and humanity, 3) the preacher is invited to tell, as a particular rhetorical form, concrete eyewitness event or story, not abstract truths, and 4) the preacher's witness is not the whole truth; the truth is always larger than what the preacher witnesses from the preacher's own limited point of view and even physical location. Thus, humility is an essential virtue of the preacher as witness.[5]

Of course, there is a noticeable hermeneutical distinction between preaching as witness and reporting. Namely, preaching as witness is more about finding God's grace working in Scripture that is applicable to the world, while reporting is more about finding God's grace in the world in light of Scripture. These two approaches are not polar opposite or mutually exclusive. Rather, some may even say that these are two sides of the same coin; the two should happen equally in any preaching. But it also rings truthful that different preaching methods have different emphases in revealing the love, care, and grace of God.[6] Witnessing can be a helpful concept for preaching as reporting.

Practical Tips

- **Select Adoption of the Seven Traits: Holistic artistry** is visible to a great extent in this style. Above all, the preacher uses hand gestures, facial expressions, and intonation to effect a holistic sermonic performance. In addition, the artistic background, other aesthetic artifacts, and the careful use of technological elements (e.g., digital sound effects) all promote the beauty and liveliness of the preached Word digitalized. The high visibility of the preaching event can enhance the **cross-cultural ubiquity** of the Word by the adoption of images, music, dancing, and other elements from different cultures and contexts.

• **Teamwork:** Collaboration with RDCs is essential in the creation of effective preaching. Ideally, RDCs should get involved in the sermon production process from the beginning. The POWER worship model may work well: Planning, Organizing, Worship/Preaching, Evaluation, and Reflection. Planning is the first stage or the brainstorming step, when the preacher and RDCs, along with other worship team members, gather together toward the basic planning of the upcoming sermon or a sermon series. Then, through the Organizing step, the whole team comes up with details of worship and preaching, such as songs, short stories or testimonies, relevant images and news clips, live performances, sound effects, the preacher's digital backgrounds, and more. The Worship/Preaching stage is what it literally means: the actual worship service and preaching practice. Then, during the Evaluation, each individual involved in the worship team, including the preacher and RDCs, does personal reflection on the performed worship and preaching, gathering thoughts and taking notes. Finally, for Reflection, the whole team gathers for the collective evaluation of the worship and preaching. This five-stage POWER model may work best as a regular four-week strategic rhythm, conjoining Evaluation and Reflection as a one-week stage.[7] The point is that RDCs should be an essential part of the whole enterprise of online worship and preaching, from the beginning stage to the end, toward the maximum fruitful utilization of the Reporter style.

- **Study News Reporting:** I'd highly recommend that preachers who want to practice the Reporter style actually watch and carefully study news reporters appearing on various daily news channels. Observe how they speak, what language they adopt, what facial expressions they make in relation to the subjects they are reporting (investigative reporting, court reporting, accident reporting, political reporting, fashion reporting, business reporting, sports reporting, etc.), how they posture their body, how they interview relevant people on the scene, what camera angles they use in what circumstances, how they incorporate different information sources into their reporting (polls, surveys, scientific data, expert opinions, etc.), what they wear, and so on. There are certain limits in applying the reporter study results to Reporter-style preaching; news reports tend not to use or rely on Scripture. Yet surely, many invaluable, practically applicable benefits will be found in the study of news reporting.

- **Sermon Writing (Who, When, Where, Why, What, How & Why):** The content of news reporting consists of the following six basic elements, namely the who, when, where, what, how, and why. Reporter-style preachers will want to write and deliver the sermon with these six reporting ingredients in order to live up to the style's unique nature. The same recommendation can apply to biblical interpretation too. When the preacher exegetes the text, on top of any usual aesthetic and historical-critical study of the text, the preacher will want to conduct a thorough analysis of the text with these six reporting aspects. There could be, of course, some significant overlap between the former and the latter, but the point is a little more intentional study of the text with the six reporting ingredients. Then, the preacher will feel more comfortable writing and delivering the sermon with the same six elements, ideally making close hermeneutical connections between the six aspects of the text and the six aspects of the world's events today.

- **Whole Worship as Witnessing/Reporting:** As the sample worship/preaching clip shows (see Figure 3), the whole worship service looks like faithful witnessing, culminating in the preacher's Reporter style message. That is, each liturgical segment of worship is designed, alongside preaching, as witness of God's grace in the world. This integrative design really helps preachers' homiletical reporting as they can make references to those collaborative witnesses in the sermon delivery. (It's like a news reporter making a reference to an expert's opinion or eyewitness testimony.) In that way, the content of the sermon and its viability is highly augmented by its liturgical surroundings and vice versa; preaching in turn affirms the witnessing of others happening in their very own *Sitz im Leben*. Again, this is why teamwork, especially with RDCs, is so important in Reporter-style preaching.

- **Flashcards:** Using flashcards with sermon outlines will be helpful for the preacher in keeping eye contact focused on the camera and generating a live and lively speaking performance. Full manuscript preaching will minimize the expected effects of the Reporter style, as there is no formal pulpit. For some preachers, the teleprompter would work very well for eye contact and lively speaking purposes. Generally, however, full manuscript preaching should be shunned.

Final Remarks

Perhaps the *media* reporting style should be the full title of this chapter. The Reporter style certainly requires virtuous maneuvering of various types of digital media, beyond the use of broadcasting cameras and online access. This means, first, that the preacher must be well-steeped in digital culture and its new—or ever-evolving—communication tools. The preacher should develop a solid, functional practical theology of digital culture. Otherwise, there is a chance that the preacher might end up chasing after one new digital media feed after another in a hurried, nonreflective application. Second, the media culture of the whole church is very important as well. If the congregants are not ready to hear messages done in the Reporter style, the preacher and RDCs' diligent collaborative homiletical work may not yield its expected fruits. The whole worship team should be well aware of their target audience's level of digital literacy and develop appropriate digital-communicative media strategies. Thankfully, we have seen many fine cases in local ecclesial communities. Let's be assiduous in learning from them—their triumphs and errors.

Other Resources

Paula Froke et al., eds., *The Associated Press Stylebook 2020-2022*, 55th ed. (New York: Associated Press, 2020).
This volume provides essential guidelines of news writing and editing around different subjects like religion, sports, health, science, business, etc., which should be very helpful in reporting-style sermon composition.

Craig Detweiler, *IGods: How Technology Shapes Our Spiritual and Social Lives* (Grand Rapids, MI: Brazos Press, 2014).
For preachers who want to better understand how communicative technology and social media function spiritually in today's world, this resource is invaluable.

Notes

1 For example, see https://www.youtube.com/watch?v=yo44NzWjp0A &feature=emb_title (accessed October 10, 2020).
2 Some preachers use the full manuscript with the help of the teleprompter.
3 For an insight on the sacramental-homiletical approach to naming God's grace out in the world, see Mary Catherine Hilkert, *Naming Grace: Preaching and the Sacramental Imagination* (New York: Continuum, 1997).

4 Frida Mannerfelt, "Co-Preaching: The Effects of Religious Digital Creatives' Engagement in the Preaching Event," *Religions* 13, no. 12 (November 23, 2022): 1–20, https://doi.org/10.3390/rel13121135.

5 Thomas G. Long, *The Witness of Preaching*, 3rd ed. (Louisville, KY: Westminster John Knox Press, 2016), 50–57.

6 As a quick example, three-point doctrinal deductive preaching and story-based inductive preaching differ in their revelation of God's grace in Scripture and the world; typically the former has more focus on Scripture and the latter more on the world or human experiences.

7 For ongoing weekly worship, the team will be at different stages of the model simultaneously for different services (e.g., reflecting on the sermon a week prior while getting ready for the upcoming worship/preaching). For churches having multiple worship teams, it could be a different story.

CHAPTER 5

The Metaverse/VR Style (Virtual Reality)

Figure 4[1]

General Description

Now preaching can and is happening even in the imaginative space of virtual reality or the metaverse. Preachers create their own digital avatars—which may even look different from them in real-life—representing themselves and preaching in virtual worship spaces while sermon listeners join the preachers with their own creative avatars. With the VR headset and hand controller on, preachers can speak to their listeners via their own voices, and their natural hand gestures and body motions are projected into the virtual reality. Soon it may also be possible to project the preacher's facial expressions. For any other creative ways of sermon delivery or sermon-associated activities (e.g., small sermon discussion groups with people around the world during or after the service), the sky's the limit. In a similar vein, with the automatic instant language translation function, preachers can reach out to people of numerous cultures and languages around the globe. Of course, a huge stumbling block toward the popularity of this metaverse or the VR-style preaching is, at least at this point, the economic unaffordability of VR gadgets for most potential congregants. The situation might change in the foreseeable future; recall the almost unapproachable price tags of old-time telephone-sized cell phones when they were first commercialized decades ago, which have gone down now to nearly universal affordability levels. Thus, who knows? We might see the VR-style preaching's popularity soon around us, which gives us a legitimate reason to explore this style.

Details of the Style

Who

As the example of DJ Soto shows (see Figure 4), the preacher typically takes on the role of pastoral DJ. What does a DJ do in general at concerts? They provide music for masses with incredible hospitality in public arenas so that the gathered may mingle with one another freely and merrily—even with total strangers. A pastoral DJ also provides both music and words in a hospitable virtual space where worshippers will mesh with extreme ease. As a matter of fact, it is likely that each week total strangers—both to the preacher and to one another—will meet through their avatars, coming out from all over the world. In that virtual environment, the preacher's hospitality is an absolute ingredient for the gathering's success. The preacher should be able to "hang out" with both strangers and regular members, along with delivering quick greetings, small talks, friendly gestures, and surely meaningful messages. Additionally, it is important that the preacher encourages worship participants toward generating more intimate community, during and after worship. Because these programs use avatars, the worshippers may not see each other's real face or stature. In that context, it is a real challenge to create a community of genuine belonging. Thus, the preacher should be a skilled DJ who can masterfully build a beloved virtual community where people can have real worshipful moments.

Why

The Metaverse style presents immediate novel merits to its audience. First, those not fond of or "allergic" to conventional religious environments like church buildings may find the virtual reality meeting space very friendly. Even when the DJ preacher designs the virtual space like a church sanctuary (creative ways of designing the church space are unlimited; the meeting space can even be different every single time), people may be less resistant, thanks to its colorful animation effects. Preachers like Daniel Herron even use online game platforms to construct the worship space, targeting younger online gamers as potential worshippers.[2] Herron's nondenominational online church has more than 15,000 members, many of whom make regular visits to his church but not necessarily to the traditional brick-and-mortar churches.

Another noticeable advantage of the Metaverse style is its truly global-interactive character. Worshippers can join the virtual faith community from all parts of the world, and their participation can be very active. Unlike Zoom or YouTube worship, by which people can also gather from around the world, in the virtual space, people can interact freely through their avatars. They can walk toward others and hug or shake hands with them, exchanging their greetings or blessings. Typically, the DJ preacher, just like in the conventional church setting, makes good use of interactional moments by approaching and befriending them before delivering the prepared message. When appropriate emoji accompany greetings, which often happens, this pastoral greeting can be both fun and highly meaningful.

Last, among many other strong merits, preachers, especially those in the early stage of their pastoral career, can begin a worshipping community with highly advantageous economic affordability. Simply put, all they need is an affordable VR headset and a small room. From that tiny space, they can construct a full-scale virtual worshipping sanctuary with congregants coming from all parts of the globe. What a world the preacher can speak to!

Where

DJ Soto drives an RV home around the country with his family, and on Sunday mornings the moving home becomes his church base from which he enters his metaverse church. He used to be a local in-person church pastor, but now the VR church is his only church. Thus, DJ Soto exemplifies that the VR church can be hosted anywhere, be it an apartment bedroom, a residential house, an RV home, a church's sanctuary, a shopping mall, or in outdoor nature, as long as there is a Wi-Fi connection. The preacher's creative construction of the virtual sanctuary matters. As a quick innovative sample, DJ Soto once constructed the Galilean seashore and created several fishing boats when he preached on a story of Mark 4:35-41, in which the disciples of Jesus experience violent winds and near-shipwreck while Jesus sleeps in the stern. DJ Soto begins the sermon in the church sanctuary and, in the middle of it, invites the sermon participants to walk to the imaginative Galilean seashore he precreated nearby. So the sermon participant avatars, alongside that of the preacher, "literally" walk to the seashore where they can see and "touch" the boat where Jesus and his disciples were. Cool, isn't it? That is exactly where the sermon culminates and people immerse themselves in the biblical story. Truly, there is no limit in terms of where preaching happens.

When

DJ Soto hosts live worship and preaching on Sunday morning, and this may work well for other VR preachers. As mentioned, the live and lively interaction between the preacher and the worshippers is essential in creating an intimate virtual community. For that purpose, live worship is the best option. Yet as long as it's live, worship can happen on any day. The preacher may even hold several worship services on weekdays, depending on the worship participants' different availability and time zones. Again, the participants can come from all parts of the globe. Thus, it would be reasonable for the preacher to accommodate different participants' different schedules.

It is good to have in mind that the VR style, like other worship services, requires plenty of preparation, especially when the preacher wants to construct different virtual worship spaces each week, depending on the week's topic and biblical text. And for those who are new to the VR style, virtual space construction is no easy task. Thus, for new VR preachers, a weekly service should suffice, while for more experienced ones, multiple times could be possible.

What

Image preaching or an image-driven sermon work best. Recall that this is virtual-space preaching. As soon as the sermon participants enter the worship space, they encounter all kinds of colorful images: avatars, natural scenes, the church sanctuary, the virtual background, emoji, and other important digital images and video clips. Preachers will want to avail themselves of these images or the image-driven space to maximize effective sermonic communication. While the preachers and their verbal communication need not compete with and win over the powerful images around the virtual space, they will want to utilize the given environment in ways that best assist their verbal communication. At times, images themselves may contribute significantly to the sermon's meaning-making. The preacher's oral/aural message and the surrounding images must not be in fierce communicational-semantic conflict or battle, but rather produce hermeneutical symbiosis in the sermon's message-making.

Useful Homiletic Theory

In her insightful volume, *Making a Scene in the Pulpit: Vivid Preaching for Visual Listeners*, Alyce M. McKenzie provides a helpful definition of "the preacher as scene maker."[3] While acknowledging the homiletical strengths of conventional narrative or story preaching, McKenzie points out that story preachers could enhance their sermons by investing more energy in and giving more hermeneutical focus to textual scenes themselves and ultimately to recreating those scenes in the sermons. More specifically, she encourages preachers to best—that is, vividly—utilize narrative characters, small yet specific textual scenes, and detailed conflicts subtly yet significantly embedded in those stories. For instance, the story of the prodigal son, according to her analysis, consists of at least six scenes that could be adopted into multiscene sermon writing and delivery: 1) the boy asking for his inheritance, 2) his squandering it in various forms of excess, 3) his decision to return home as he sits with pigs, 4) his trip home rehearsing what he will say to his father, 5) his father's greeting, and 6) his father's encounter with the old brother.[4]

The same principle applies to seeing or showing various congregational contexts of life. Preachers are to notice vivid scenic aspects of their listeners' lives and incorporate them into sermon writing in tandem with imaginative textual scenes as a critical and visual hermeneutical-dialogical process between the two. McKenzie believes that this process will lead to compelling deliverance of vivid preaching for visual listeners today.

McKenzie's insights and suggestions are particularly helpful to the VR-style preacher. As aforementioned, preachers will, more often than not, take on the role of the virtual space architect who constructs the worship space and biblical-textual scenes where they can lead participants in real time during the sermon delivery. This whole construction enterprise is to begin with the preacher's careful noticing of textual scenes and congregational life scenes and eventual reconstructing of them in the virtual space, all of which will ultimately be reflected in the verbal and performative communication of the sermon.

In resonance with McKenzie, I encourage preachers to consider the novel concept of architectural preaching, which specifically targets sermon-designing on architectural biblical passages. Such passages as Gen. 11:4, 1 Kgs. 6:1–10, 2 Chr. 3:1–17, Ezra 3:7–13, Neh. 3,Ps. 118:22, Prov. 24:3–4, Isa. 54:11–12, Jer. 22:13–14, Ezek. 42:1–20, Matt. 21:42, Luke 6:48–49, 1Cor. 3:10–13, Eph. 2:19–22, Heb 11:10, and Rev 21:9–22 lend themselves well.[5] Practically and briefly speaking, architectural preaching is centered around a) reading texts with architectural sensibility and spirituality and then b) designing the sermon spatially. Thus, conceptually, the sermon structure does not flow from Introduction to Body One, Body Two, Body Three, and so forth, and then onto the Conclusion. Instead, the sermon flows, or moves, from Sermon Entrance to Space F (front), to Space R (right), to Space L (left), Space C (center), and so forth, and then finally Sermon Backdoor. For instance,[6] when preaching on Revelation 21:9–22, the preacher can walk through the entrance of the New Jerusalem (e.g., saying, "Please follow me along into the fascinating vision of God's new Jerusalem") and move around it together with the sermon listeners, making interpretive and contemporary comments on various aspects of the heavenly architecture. It would surely make a compelling sermon, visually and somatically—though in imagination.

When VR preaching adopts this architectural homiletic, the sermon viewer's experience of architectural preaching can be accomplished not only in imagination but in reality—that is, virtual reality. Thus, for instance, the preacher can now literally walk with the sermon participant avatars through the entrance of New Jerusalem and around it while conversing about their encounter with that heavenly architecture. In this way, VR preaching can be achieved on a whole different level of dialogical reciprocity and interactive performance.

In sum, engaging the human sensory capacities of seeing, touching, feeling, and tasting beyond only hearing during the sermon event is a novel possibility and a huge merit of the VR-style preaching. Preliminary homiletical theories are already ready to assist the fine execution of the unlimited possibilities and advantages of VR preaching.

Practical Tips

- **Select Adoption of the Seven Traits:** Among others, **holistic artistry** and **multilateral spontaneous communication** are digital-liturgical hallmarks of the VR Metaverse-style preaching. In a literal sense, there is *no limit* to creating holistic experiences of preaching in terms of calligraphic fonts, colorful images, object or avatar movements, various geometrical or mathematical figures, cartoon drawings, photos, video clips, filmed natural scenes, photos, videos, music, lines, graphs, emoji, and so on. All these and more can be closely woven toward the sermon's *vivid* meaning-making. Like the Reporter style, the VR style may need a supporting tech team (e.g., RDCs) who can collaborate with the preacher from sermon brainstorming to sermon performance. Yet unlike the Reporter style, which typically requires the tech team's presence during live preaching, the preacher of the VR style, like DJ Soto, could manage the whole tech dimension of preaching without the team's assistance, as long as the preacher is well versed in digital culture and well-equipped with online tech skills.

Multilateral and multicultural spontaneous communication is the bloodstream of VR-style preaching. People can come to the worship service from every corner of the globe, and so long as their language skills allow (this is totally possible these days, thanks to the automatic translation function), the preacher and the international sermon participants can communicate instantly and richly. Before, during, and after the sermon, their conversations may continue through various multimedia tools as specified above; for instance, sermon participants can share their photos relevant to the day's key topic right in the middle of the sermon. All this—lively and meaningful engagement of the sermon by multitudes—could be preachers' dreams come true!

- **Explore the Metaverse (Make Friends):** VR-style preaching is more than purchasing a VR headset and delivering a weekly message in this novel animated reality. Equally important is an in-depth exploration of the metaverse as a whole and a fine sense of how it is experienced. First, preachers may want to understand *why* people are *in* the metaverse. What draws people into the metaverse world beyond the physical one? What differences in life do we experience in the metaverse? What do we want to experience that we cannot in physical reality? Or what do we want to *not* experience in the metaverse? These questions become important as preachers prepare themselves for the VR-style preaching and worship space. One of the easiest and most effective ways to navigate the questions is making friendly visits to VR streets, beaches, concerts, and shopping malls, making friends there coming from many parts of the globe, and having meaningful chats with them. Do this before launching the VR church or the VR preaching event, or continue to do so during weekdays if the VR ministry continues. The metaverse itself continually changes in terms of the user base, space design, item availability, methods of people's connection, and so forth. Preachers better know those changes and people's adaptive responses to them as part of their continued pastoral research on sermon participants.

- **Establishing a Beloved Community:** As in the brick-and-mortar church, community building cannot be overemphasized in effective VR-style preaching. Put bluntly, where there is excellent community fellowship, the community better hears the message. We tend to think that genuine community building is far more limited, if not impossible, on digital online platforms. Nay. For good or ill, during the Covid-19 pandemic, we experienced the high possibility of marvelous community fellowship on online platforms such as Zoom, YouTube, Google Meet, and Facebook Rooms, and still many churches use various apps to stay connected with their congregations. VR-style preachers, therefore, can and should invest in establishing beloved communities among their worship participants beyond their Sunday morning proclamation. For instance, they could lead weekly gathering activities or monthly hangout activities. Believe it or not, online gaming together works well for a certain group of (church) people to build a trusted community. A youth pastor in Newberg, Oregon, for example, has a portion of the official church budget specifically designated for purchasing online games. He said the church budget committee happily approved the budget as they understand sound online gaming really helps community building among youth.
- **Face-to-Face on Zoom:** It is certainly true, at least at this moment of technological development, that in the VR church people cannot see the real faces of the worship participants, rather only 3D images

of avatars. Some people greatly appreciate this anonymity as they may meet total strangers whom they may not trust in the virtual space. Some others, however, look for opportunities to connect with real people behind the avatars. Thus, why not host voluntary face-to-face hangouts on Zoom or other platforms from time to time outside of the virtual worship context? That way, people and the preacher will have a great chance to meet up with their real selves, establishing a different level of holy intimacy and friendship among virtual churchgoers.

- **Dialogical Q&A Preaching:** As multilateral spontaneous communication is possible and desired in the VR style, the dialogical Q&A design of preaching is highly recommended. Of course, this does not mean the whole sermon is the complete set of the preacher's answers to the questions from the sermon participants, though this could be possible and tried on rare occasions. Rather, consider sharing big sermon-relevant questions at the beginning and the end. Then, the preacher may want to allow a couple of minutes or so for the sermon participants themselves to have a chat on the questions either via text chat or one-on-one speaking. When they come back, the preacher may answer any follow-up questions from the sermon participants or make a quick comment on the original questions and move on. Alternatively, the preacher may drop questions on major sermon transitions, including the introduction and conclusion, and make continuous comments along the way to chat texts or emoji from the sermon participants—yes, the sermon participants would be more than happy to respond with a variety of emoji to the preacher's questions rather than via typed texts or verbal talks.

- **Special Ministry for Older Adults:** There is a serious generational myth or bias that virtual reality in general, and VR-style preaching in particular, only work well with the MZ (millennials and Gen Z) or younger generations. Totally misguided. As the popularity of smartphones and SNS apps among those in their 50s and beyond shows, Boomers and the elderly of the Silent generation are also in love with digitized *human* communication. True, at this point, the VR user base is limited among those older generations, but there is a huge audience waiting for the preacher's gentle and caring outreach. Thus, why not a special VR preaching ministry for older people?

Final Remarks

All that has been said above may sound a bit (or largely!) rosy. The national or global user base is still limited, partly to the high price of the headset and for other reasons like the metaverse's slender popularity, at least for now. Also, as Daniel Herron's case shows,[7] there are issues around theological legitimacy. Herron started the virtual church as a teenager with no formal theological training or degree; at one point, his church had 15,000 members. Is this phenomenon acceptable? To whom? Certainly, not to conventional denominational churches. But again, as DJ Soto has made it clear, interested people are making frequent visits to his VR church and experiencing meaningful life in faith through fellowship with faithful people. DJ Soto began his VR church even before the start of the Covid-19 pandemic and still leads it. Thus, there is no doubt that the VR church and its preaching have an undeniable raison d'être to which we must give our keen attention before it is too late.

Other Resources

Matthew Ball, *The Metaverse: And How It Will Revolutionize Everything*, 1st ed. (New York: Liveright Publishing Corporation, 2022).

This volume provides a comprehensive understanding of the metaverse, from its origin and general introduction to how to build a metaverse space and to predictions of the future of the ever-evolving metaverse.

Darrell L. Bock and Jonathan J. Armstrong, *Virtual Reality Church: Pitfalls and Possibilities* (Chicago: Moody, 2021).

Among other helpful content in this volume, notable is a thorough biblical-theological appreciation of virtual reality, which is rare in the market now.

Notes

1 "Going to Church in Virtual Reality," CNN, assessed February 27, 2023, https://www.cnn.com/videos/us/2018/11/13/going-to-church-in-virtual-reality-beme.beme.

2 "Going to Church in Virtual Reality."

3 McKenzie, *Making a Scene in the Pulpit: Vivid Preaching for Visual*, 5.

4 McKenzie, *Making a Scene in the Pulpit: Vivid Preaching for Visual* , 4

5 Sunggu A. Yang, "With Jørn Utzon: Approaching and Preaching Architectural Texts," *Homiletic* 45, no. 2 (2020): 53–69.

6 Read the referred open-access article for details. (Yang, "With Jørn Utzon: Approaching and Preaching Architectural Texts.")

7 Watch the CNN clip in footnote 1.

CHAPTER 6

The Interview Style

Figure 5[1]

General Description

This is one of the friendliest styles of online preaching, along with the Zoom/Chat style explored later. In most cases, the preacher sets up in an environment that is absent of any religious symbols or references. The preacher may sit at home in the living room or in the flowery backyard of the church grounds. Usually, a calm atmosphere is favored as a sermonic "interview" is being held. This style creates the feeling of participation in an interview between the preacher and sermon viewers. The conversation proceeds in a dialogical manner with the preacher providing answers to presumed questions from sermon listeners, much like a pastoral mentor in their midst; note that it is the preacher alone who speaks during the whole sermon. To promote this effect, the sermon often utilizes actual questions and answers with moments of expressed humility when the preacher may say, "I don't actually have an answer for that" or "I may need more time to think about what you've asked me on today's sermon text." Finally, in order to create the feel of a real interview, two or three cameras focus on the preacher from different angles throughout the sermon.

Details of the Style

Who

The preacher should present as a humble, yet expert, life mentor based on friendly commentary on a given text and topic. To borrow Thomas Long's terminology, the Interview-style preacher's image is pastor rather than herald or poet/storyteller. As Long articulates, this preacher would "intentionally seek a beneficial change in the hearers, should help people make sense of their lives and should strive to be a catalyst for more responsible and ethical living on the part of those who hear."[2] This pastor is not assertive in voice, message, or posture, nor does the pastor impose things—hard doctrinal beliefs—on the sermon reviewers. Rather, the message should be invitational, conversational, and highly pastoral, showing genuine care and concern over people's various life issues: relationship problems, unexpected suffering, important turning points of life, and the like. The preacher will appear as an approachable friend, mentor, counselor, and fellow pilgrim. Thus, the preacher would rarely don explicit religious symbolism like a traditional liturgical robe. As the sample shows, a comfortable pair of jeans or long-sleeve polo would serve well as the preacher's usual Sunday outfit. Of course, cultural or generational context will determine what is informal or formal. Preacher still should be able to present themselves as professional experts in the matter of Christian faith and as a faithful sages for public online broadcasting in their pastoral manner and communication skills.

Why

The Interview style is best suited for the preacher's or the church's friendly outreach to unchurched or religious seekers, or today's typical Spiritual-But-Not-Religious audiences (SBNR). Homiletic methodology, this style is innovative and appealing. Before the 1970s, deductive- or herald-style preaching had been a mainstay; up until around the 2010s, inductive preaching or narrative preaching was a popular homiletical modus operandi and still has lingering popularity.

The Interview style distinguishes itself from the formality of both. The herald mode of communication is assertive, and conventional inductive preaching often builds upon a tension-resolution narrative and culminates in the attention-drawing "Aha!" moment at the end of the sermon. In contrast, the Interview style continually offers important insights and opinions about life and God along the way. This style may generate several or many small "Aha" moments here and there in the sermon. In that sense, the Interview style is both innovative and appealing to today's highly diverse and democratic listening body of the church and the unchurched. Seekers or SBNR-ers especially appreciate multifaceted conversational teaching rather than top-down imposing messages—many churches these days have even adopted the term *teaching* over *preaching*. Also, they give their listening ears more easily to readily comprehensible, though certainly not cheap, insights about life and God rather than a prolonged sermonic narrative built on one big universal idea. For seekers or SBNR-ers, universal is almost synonymous with assertive.

Additionally, the Interview style can jack up the sermon viewers' attention and engagement level. This is the *Interview* style because the sermon flows as if the sermon viewers interview the preacher. In that respect, bluntly speaking, the Interview style loses all its homiletical rationale without the sermon viewers' active engagement (which will be discussed further below in Practical Tips). Hence, the ideal execution of the Interview style will surely guarantee the heightened attention level of the sermon viewers.

Where

As the sample illustration shows, the church's fellowship hall or the preacher's home living room or study close to translucent windows is an ideal place. The church's main worship hall might be a good candidate, too, but as said above, it is better to evade explicit religious symbolism; choose somewhere that is friendly, approachable, and highly daily life-relevant. An important caveat is that the background of the preacher must not be overwhelming or too visual in order not to dwarf the preacher's physical presence. As this is the *Interview* style, the whole environment should be engineered to assist the viewers' focus on the preacher. This is a big visual-semantic difference between the Interview style and the Reporter style. In the Reporter style, certain visuals (e.g., photos, video clips, live performances) should take a central place in terms of the sermon flow, or at least be juxtaposed with major sermon points with equal weight. This shouldn't be so with the Interview style. The preacher might want to use certain props during the message, but those props should remain secondary.

As for space arrangement, a simple, comfortable chair or a desk—behind which the preacher sits staring at the camera—should suffice. Unlike the Conversation style, a digital curtain or CGI background creation (Computer Graphic Image) is not recommended. It is imperative that the preacher's live "interview" feels very natural with no artificial sophistication. Authenticity and truthfulness greatly matter for the Interview style.

When

Live streaming is highly recommended—if not required. Again, authenticity and truthfulness greatly matter for the Interview style. Sermon reviewers much appreciate the preacher interviewee's unfiltered, unedited, and thus live speech at the scheduled time. This does not mean, of course, that preaching has always to happen on Sunday morning. It could be Sunday evening, Saturday morning, Friday afternoon, or on many other occasions, as long as preaching is done in real time through the advertised schedule and the worship team, including the camera crew, is available.

What

Testimony may serve as the best description of what to say in the practice of the Interview style. As an interviewee or testifier, the preacher goes not preach to the people out there, but rather *shares with* them the preacher's faithful witness of God or personal meditative thoughts on the text. Particularly, sermon viewers would like to hear how the friendly, approachable preacher wisely links the ancient text with daily life. It is not likely that the preacher will have all the answers that the viewers bring to the sermon moment—nor would they expect that. What they would like to hear is the preacher's honest thoughts on or struggles with the text that may sometimes make sense and at other times may not. It is as if the sermon viewers are asking, "What do *you* think and feel about the text as *a simple human being like me* (yet, of course, with your own wisdom and insights as a teacher and mentor)?" In this aspect, Phillips Brooks' time-proven homiletical axiom, "truth through [sound] personality," seems to make perfect sense. Who the preacher is—that is, the sound human character with respectful virtues—matters as an essential part of what is being said. The preacher's testimony should be authentic, genuine, and truthful.

However, as an important note, all this does not mean that the sermon content of the Interview style is all about the preacher's personal—or worse, private—thoughts on the text, with no serious study. Quite the contrary. What is required of testimonial preaching is the preacher's diligent study of the text, a deeper encounter of the Spirit within the text, and finally any personal, full, hermeneutical digestion of the study and encounter. Only then will the dialogue provided during the sermonic interview be richer and Spirit-full. Simply put, the sermonic interview is not a time for cheap spiritual pep talk, but for text-engaging sage conversation.

For the interview conversation to be engaging and relevant, ideally sermon viewers will actually study the same sermon passage and send questions to the preacher days ahead or weeks earlier, if possible. Then, the preacher would incorporate them into the sermon preparation as fit. Of course, the preacher would not have to always rely on questions from the viewers. The preacher may also like to create such imaginative and dialogical questions as, "Now as you hear my message more today, you may wonder, 'Is it right?' That's the same question I had when I was first reading the text for today. Let me share my answers as honestly as possible for you before we depart." Throughout the sermon, the preacher may want to move back and forth between asking questions and fielding questions from the viewers.

Useful Homiletic Theory

Anna Florence in *Preaching as Testimony* provides a biblical-theologically well-informed concept of testimony which aligns with the Interview style's use of the same term. Florence defines testimony as "both a narration of events and a confession of belief,"[3] beyond testimony as merely telling one's own story or narrating personal illustrations. Specifically, she claims, the testimonial preacher will tell "what she has seen and heard *in the biblical text and in life*, and then confess what she believes about it" (italics original).[4] One can with ease find the fine application of Florence-defined testimony in the Black homiletical tradition. Recall Dr. Martin Luther King Jr. saying during his very last sermon, the day before his assassination, "[God] has allowed me to go up to the mountaintop. And I have looked over. I have seen the promised land. I may not get there with you. But I want you to know tonight that we as a people get to the promised."[5] In this testimonial sermon, Dr. King stated he *has seen and heard* what happened in the biblical text as if he had been actually there when Moses and ancient Israelites camped just on the opposite side of the Jordan River, looking over the land flowing with milk and honey. What is important is that Dr. King states it in the present tense, which means he is still seeing it and hearing it and eventually living it out as his own. That is why, as Richard Lischer shared, during the life of Dr. King, his comrades and followers considered him "a new Moses,"[6] participating in Dr. King–created testimonial reality as their own. The Interview preacher does the same. The preacher offers a biblical-theological testimony of life in the present tense and invites sermon viewers' active participation into the divine-sanctioned story world, which is not a fake one at all but very much real: "I have seen the promised land!"

Jerusha M. Neal sheds an additional insight in her sophisticated articulation of Mary's testimonial song as preaching found in Luke. This is her proclamatory song as recorded:

And Mary said,

"My soul magnifies the Lord,
 and my spirit rejoices in God my Savior,
for he has looked with favor on the lowly state of his
 servant.
 Surely from now on all generations will call me
 blessed,
for the Mighty One has done great things for me,
 and holy is his name;
indeed, his mercy is for those who fear him
 from generation to generation.
He has shown strength with his arm;
 he has scattered the proud in the imagination of
 their hearts.
He has brought down the powerful from their thrones
 and lifted up the lowly;
he has filled the hungry with good things
 and sent the rich away empty.
He has come to the aid of his child Israel,
 in remembrance of his mercy,
according to the promise he made to our ancestors,
 to Abraham and to his descendants forever."
  (Luke 1:46-55, NRSVUE)

The whole chapter is a testimonial conversation between Mary and Elizabeth—actually, Mary's response to Elizabeth's blessings upon her. It is as if Elizabeth and Mary are sitting face-to-face and asking (or interviewing!) each other's reasons for hope and joy ("Mary, what really happened to you when the angel made a visit to you?" and "Elizabeth, is it true that your husband has been unable to speak during your whole pregnancy?"), and finally answering each other's curiosity with such blessings. Neal, in particular, sees Mary's Magnificat as testimonial preaching full of a Spirit-overshadowed individual's proclamation of justice, love, and radical hospitality to the broken, hungry world.[7] Mary *has seen and heard and preaches*, just like the Interview style preacher.

Practical Tips

- **Select Adoption of the Seven Traits:** The pastoral and interview feel of preaching comes with the traits of **usability** and **connectivity** of the Word digitalized. Scripture becomes a fine hermeneutical catalyst for the deeper homiletical interview process (thus good usability of Scripture is demonstrated), and listeners as invisible yet influential interviewers may experience a close connection with the pastoral testimonial partner. Holistic artistry may also be experienced in this style by matching the surrounding environment modestly—as mentioned, the background must not overwhelm the preacher's testimonial event—with the key theme of the sermon or Scripture. The preacher's body posture and clothing may also match the sermon's theme and similarly reflect the holistic artistry of this style.

- **Mock Interview:** There is a chance that the first-time practitioner of the Interview style may overtly tiptoe or feel like walking on thin ice during the live delivery of the sermon. A simple yet effective solution? Do a mock interview or a trial run. Once questions are collected from the congregation and preparation is complete, the preacher may want to practice with the church staff. This will surely better prepare the preacher, lowering some uncertainty and anxiety. We should not see this trial run as damaging the sermon's authenticity or the preacher's truthfulness. On the contrary, it is a well-known piece of advice that preachers, whether aspiring or seasoned, should do a pre-event practice before the actual delivery. James Forbes, one of the greatest preachers of Riverside Church, New York, used to practice his upcoming sermon, putting his head toward the Hudson River through the church's windows and shouting into the air. Common wisdom among fine preachers is that preaching gets better and the preacher even can feel more freedom during actual delivery after enough time in the trial run. The same surely applies to the Interview style.
- **Use the Lectionary Strategically:** Using the lectionary is helpful for the effective engagement of sermon viewers, as well as for rich(er) daily life-relevant content in the sermon. With the lectionary, the sermon viewers can already know what text the preacher will use for the upcoming message and be easily encouraged to read it ahead and send questions to the preacher. The church office may want to create a

shared Google Doc or something similar so congregants can make comments on the text throughout the week. If the lectionary can be used strategically, the office could share the Google Doc with the texts that will be preached on for the next two or three months, through each season of the church calendar (e.g., Lent), and encourage the people to leave their comments or questions on the document while reading several relevant texts altogether. The church can do the same for a special series of sermons (e.g., a five-week sermon series on divine-human relationship)—simply yet purposefully let people know there is a group of texts that they may enjoy for the coming weeks in dialogical interactions with the preacher.

As a side note, yes, thanks to the online bilateral communicative technology usable during the preaching event, sermon viewers may want to throw their questions and comments to the preacher in real time so the preacher may answer them. However, this practice of real-time questioning is not really desirable or encouraged. It allows very little time for the preacher to prepare properly. As we will discuss later, real-time questioning is better suited for the Zoom/Chat style, for which informality is a kind of virtue and expectation. The Interview style should feel in between formality and informality (i.e., semi-formal).

- **Impersonation:** As a creative subtype of the Interview style, the preacher may impersonate a biblical character and be interviewed as the biblical character.

For instance, the preacher may appear as Esther, saying at the beginning of the sermon, "I'm Esther, and I'd like to share my hidden story with you all this morning. You may really wonder why I did... Actually, during my lifetime, I was asked about..." Just like that, the preacher as Esther would begin the sermon with presumed questions from the sermon viewers or ancient people around her who would have been curious about her life and behavior. In order to carry out the impersonation uninterrupted by out-of-character introductions, it's helpful to have a quick caption slide, such as "An Interview with Esther Imagined," displayed on the screen before the sermon begins.

- **Two-Person Style:** As another creative subtype of the Interview style, two-person preaching is possible. Either two copreachers or a preacher with an interviewer-congregant will chat in the interview mode. The Interview style is primarily done by the preacher alone, practically speaking, to minimize any confusion and not to burden others with preaching preparation duties. But from time to time, this creative variation would work well as an attempt to elevate sermon viewers' participation and even their ownership of the preaching event; that is, sermon viewers are no longer merely passive "viewers" of the sermon.

- **Talk From Notes Only:** For purposes of the live interview feel and authenticity in front of the camera, do not have a full script in hand while preaching.

Full-script preaching can demonstrate authenticity, and of course, writing up the whole script is very much necessary for full preparation. Yet when it comes to actual delivery in this particular style, have only minimum notes in hand—no more than one or two pages. Smaller flashcards as a memory aid would help too.

- **Simple, Friendly Props:** Simple—very simple—props may work, provided they do not divert the sermon viewers' attention. For instance, for Easter, a charming small basket of eggs would make the interview environment more friendly and meaningful. For Pentecost, a thin red fabric that runs across the windows would be great. For Lent, a plate of ashes on a table in front of the preacher would be a definite yes.

Final Remarks

Due to the highly dialogical character of the Interview style, it can be confused with the Conversational style. They distinguish themselves from each other at least on two levels. First, in the Conversational style, the preacher, more often than not, poses rhetorical or actual interpretive, life-relevant questions *for* the sermon viewers (though the other way around is possible). In the Interview style, however, as discussed, the sermon viewers will bring their questions to the preacher, to which the preacher provides potential answers. Second, the Conversational style focuses more on the life situations of the sermon viewers. In the Interview style, the preacher's testimonial stories or claims are more important. For these reasons and others, the Interview style presents its own strong merits and different communicational skills required to practice it well. Certain occasions are especially well suited to the Interview style—for example, when a congregation has welcomed a "strange" pastor as their newly installed one for the church, or they would like to know more about the preacher's personal journey in faith or testimonial witness of faith.

Other Resources

Jacqueline Sharer Robertson, *Women in the Wings: 20 Biblical Monologues* (Lima, OH: CSS Publishing, 2006).
  Readers meet twenty biblical women who, by the author's imagination and as if they were being interviewed, narrate their own versions of biblical events that occurred in their lives.
Robert Taylor, *Media Interview Techniques: A Complete Guide to Media Training* (London: Kogan Page, 2016).
  A communications expert provides a practical guide to preparing for, conducting, and evaluating the result of media interviews across a range of platforms—TV, radio, internet, and video.

Notes

1 Here is an online preaching example for this style, https://www.youtube.com/watch?time_continue=3464&v=OBGNTys_Qsk&feature=emb_title (accessed October 10, 2020).
2 Long, *The Witness of Preaching*, 31.
3 Anna Carter Florence, *Preaching as Testimony*, 1st ed. (Louisville, KY: Westminster John Knox Press, 2007), xiii.
4 Florence, *Preaching as Testimony*.

5 "Martin Luther King's Last Speech: I've Been to the Mountaintop," accessed December 26, 2022, https://www.youtube.com/watch?v=zgVrlx68v-0&t=3s.

6 Richard Lischer, *The Preacher King: Martin Luther King Jr. and the Word That Moved America* (New York: Oxford University Press, 1997), 268.

7 Jerusha Matsen Neal, *The Overshadowed Preacher: Mary, the Spirit, and the Labor of Proclamation* (Grand Rapids MI: Eerdmans, 2020), chaps. 4–6.

CHAPTER 7

The Drama Style

Figure 6[1]

General Description

Many preachers in children's or youth ministry should be familiar with this style, which involves creating a physio-holistic
encounter between the preached Word and listeners that utilizes more than just verbal communication. In the Drama style,
which we might also term the Animated Prop Style, preachers
may perform a Scriptural drama in front of the camera using
necessary artifacts or props in front of the camera, or perhaps perform a drama without the preacher's appearance in a
medium like puppetry, broadcasting the scene to its target audience. Because the audience's attention span is relatively short on
the digital screen, the performance should be highly riveting to
retain attention. The sermon as drama does not have to be *overly*
spectacular; preaching is not a place for cinematic extravaganzas.

The impactful content of the gospel is still most important for the given audience. As the paraphrased words of Paul reminds us, "For the kingdom of God depends not on [spectacles] but on power" (1 Corinthians 4:20). It should also be noted that the Drama style is not exclusively for younger generations. A well-planned Scriptural drama with sophisticated props or a prefilmed dramatic sermon will serve adults as well as younger audiences. People of all ages are now living through an image-driven era.[2] Lastly, the Drama style is different from the Artist style, which will be discussed in the last chapter; the Artist style could include theatrical drama performance, but also moves far beyond it with many other ways of being artistic, such as Scripture-inspired painting or dancing. Drama style preaching presents dramas produced *through animated props*, while theatrical drama performance in the Artist style is more about the preacher's own acting of biblical characters.

Details of the Style

Who

The preacher's role is threefold: creative interpreter, drama director, and storytelling performer. When creating a drama out of a biblical text, creative or imaginative interpretation of the text is essential. After all, the Bible is not a drama or movie script, and thus does not provide enough details of biblical stories to be translated into dramas without interpretive work. Translation or dramatization of the stories is, therefore, the preacher's prime task for this style. Once the primary work of dramatization—in other words, production of the script—is completed, the preacher needs to put on the hat of the drama director to prepare and execute the full performative setting. For instance, the preacher, along with a drama team (if the church has one), would recruit performers, purchase props, set up drama stages, borrow costumes and other accessories, select music, invite makeup artist volunteers from the congregation, and so on. Last, but not least, the preacher should come across as a master storyteller or performer. To be clear, the preacher and other performers do not need to have professional training in acting, nor try to sound like a professional performer. Sermon viewers even would not expect it from the preacher. Rather, they would like to see the preacher and others presenting their characters with deep sympathy, empathy, passion, authenticity, and compassion. If the preacher sincerely embodies the sayings, emotions, and thoughts of biblical characters, sermon reviewers will be tolerant and still be truly graced.

Why

There is an interesting book in the market titled *The Rise of the Image, the Fall of the Word* by NYU professor Mitchell Stephens. As the title indicates, the main argument of the book is that in today's world, images, symbols, videos, and photos are replacing words as the primary communication medium. Given that the book was published in 1998, which was slightly before the Dot.com revolution and the recent smartphone epoch, Stephens seems to have been a social prophet. In the book, he notes, *"Perhaps we will soon locate our video at sites on the World Wide Web."* A few years later, YouTube appeared.

With Stephen's prophecy fulfilled to a great extent today, Drama-style preaching should be the preacher's faithful, timely service to the online audience, whose main digital communications are carried out not just through words, but also through images, symbols, videos, and photos. The Drama style can provide practically unlimited kinds of symbolic images and bodily performances each time when adopted for preaching. More than others, the Drama style can be effective in bringing biblical-theological images and symbols to life so that the sermon viewers actually see and feel them. For instance, it is way more inspirational and pedagogically effective to show something tangible when the preacher delivers a message on Solomon's temple or John the Seer's vision of a New Heaven and a New Earth rather than merely providing verbal descriptions of them.

Another merit of the Drama style, particularly in terms of images, is the possibility of de-westernizing the cultural orientation of the sermon viewers. It is no secret that in the West, as well as in the East, the biblical world and its characters are very much westernized to the extent that, for instance, Jesus mostly appears in films and cartoons as a blond-haired Swedish American. Thus, at times, if not most of the time, we tend to forget or simply ignore the biblical world's Middle Eastern origins and their cultural impact on biblical writings and figures, not to mention Jesus himself, who would probably have been brown skinned with dark hair. The Drama style, by the wise use of appropriate props or costumes imbued with keen multicultural awareness (for example, using Jesus figurines imported from the Middle East), can help de-westernize the biblical world and people's perception of it.

Where

This style does not require a formal sanctuary setting, though that isn't totally undesirable. Rather, a fellowship hall or a decent Sunday school classroom should suffice. Depending on the local church's digital capacity, the worship team may want to create a green screen-based digital background relevant to the day's sermon. The digital background, however, is only an option. The chosen space's wall—whatever color it may have—with simple decorative work should work perfectly well. If necessary, the preacher's church office or even the preacher's home living room can be utilized as well, as long as the space is well aligned with or enhances the sermon's message. For certain occasions, outdoor space is also good (e.g., when preaching on Genesis 1).

It is critical to note that all these spaces are *secondary* ones in terms of the sermon's meaning-making and the sermon viewer's perception of the preaching space. The *primary* spaces are the ones that the preacher and the worship team create around the drama table or the stage they adopt for each sermon. See the sample (Figure 5). The preacher sets up a drama table with simple yet efficient decoration—probably any table from the classroom!—and preaches from there. For this sermon, the prime preaching space is not the room itself but the table. The drama table is the *sanctuary and pulpit.* The same is true with sermon viewers. They will see the table as the sanctuary and pulpit. Thus, the preacher should feel both freedom and solemnity when choosing where preaching takes place. Almost anything or everything (e.g., a dining room table!) can be chosen, but at the same time, we should remember that through and around *that anything* the Word of the Lord speaks—namely, the very Word of healing, restoration, and ultimate hope for humanity.

When

Unlike most other online preaching styles discussed thus far, prerecording of the sermon is better for the Drama style than live presentation due to simple yet reasonable liturgical-logistic matters. As discussed, the Drama style requires its own creative space and key props associated with it. This drama/pulpit space might not fit well with other worship components, at least in terms of space use. As the sample sermon clip of figure 6 shows (follow its endnote link), other worship components, like worship dancing or prayer, do not necessarily take place around the drama table. First, this could simply be inconvenient in terms of space rearrangement and, second, a bit confusing due to the potential multiple uses of a drama table that is specifically designed for a particular story of the sermon. The worship team and the preacher will record different portions of the liturgy at different times and edit them all as a whole liturgy. This means that like the VR style and the Reporter style, the Drama style requires a close collaboration and well-planned time management between the preacher and the worship team. If Sunday morning is the target broadcasting time, it is ideal that all prerecordings happen by Friday afternoon, so that the church's digital staff may work on the editing on Saturday. Some understaffed churches might have to do all prerecordings and editing on Saturday, morning to afternoon, as staff or volunteers would not be available during the weekdays. This should be certainly possible with a small-scale Drama style of preaching.

What

Like the VR style, the Drama style is best done as image preaching or an image-driven sermon. Yet, a notable difference of the Drama style, for its name's sake, is its *performed drama*. There will be characters (other drama performers can be recruited alongside the preacher), dialogue, narrative plot, music as necessary, spectacle, central theme, and so forth. Thus, sermons on biblical stories are typical. Yet, the Drama style is possible not only through narrative texts (e.g., the book of Esther or parables of Jesus), but also through doctrinal ones. For instance, through the "wild" imagination of the preacher, the preacher could come up with a quick fictional or realistic story in Romans 10:12: "For there is no distinction between Jew and Greek; the same Lord is Lord of all and is generous to all who call on him." In the story, the preacher could perform an imaginative friendly dialogue between a Jew and a Greek.

Naturally, the sermon script will take the form of a drama script. The script will have character conversations, pieces of third-person narration, notes for performances, directions for the camera angle, an introduction or conclusion of the drama if necessary, and the like. This sermon writing certainly will require a different orientation of sermon composition; for one thing, this is not essay writing but literary writing. This will be more discussed below in Useful Homiletic Theory and Practical Tips.

As an additional note, it is a mistake to think that writing the sermon script in the form of a drama script is easier and does not really require hard-worked exegesis. On the contrary. As the finest novelists or drama script writers know, only diligent research on the subject and topic guarantees great writing. The same is true with sermon script writing. Only industrious study of the text will guarantee fine sermon script writing for the Drama style. Otherwise, the sermon script could become too fictional, full of the preacher's own exegetical thoughts or read-into ideologies. In sum, the Drama style preacher is doubly tasked, both to do the hard study *and* produce an insightful and exciting drama script. This could be much harder work, though of course with plenty of joy and rewarding moments.

Useful Homiletic Theory

The Drama style preaching in general is not conventional; that is, it is not typical pulpit preaching, which is more traditional and much more familiar to practicing preachers. This is the same with the congregants. Mostly, they are accustomed to preachers speaking (alone) from the pulpit or stage, without visible material artifacts and props. How can the whole church, then, including the preacher, be reoriented—of course if they desire to be so—to become more Drama style preaching-friendly? Anna Carter Florence in her *Rehearsing Scripture: Discovering God's Word in Community* provides an excellent solution to that contextual question. Even better, her solution is solidly theatrical and homiletical theory-driven, yet very practical with step-by-step instructions. To be clear, her approach is not designed specifically for the Drama style we're discussing, namely, the production of the animated drama sermon with visible artifacts. Her proposal is more about the preacher and the congregants exploring biblical texts theatrically or in her own words as "the repertory church" before the actual sermon design and writing. The preacher then will speak (alone) on Sunday morning. With that considered, her proposal is still helpful for the Drama style. First, her method helps the whole church familiarize itself with the dramatization of the biblical text. And second, very importantly, she helps us read or "rehearse" biblical texts in dramatized ways, which must be a firm foundation for the practice of Drama style preaching.

Among many useful lessons from her book, her instructions on reading and dramatizing verbs of biblical texts stand out as very helpful for the Drama style, and specifically the style's sermon script writing. She realizes that studying and dramatizing verbs carefully can lead to an in-depth, real-life understanding of biblical characters and their faith contexts. Below are her ten suggestions on how to theatrically explore verbs:[3]

- Who gets what verbs?
- What's the order of those verbs?
- What do the verb tense and mood tell you?
- What do the verbs stir or evoke in you? What do you remember about them from the times you and or others have played them?
- Are these verbs associated with certain groups or people? Are they used to stereotype or make broad generalizations?
- If you run the verbs through your biblical echo chamber, what do you hear?
- If God is a character in this verse, how are God's verbs different from others?
- Do any of the verbs surprise you? Why? What were you expecting?
- Did you spot any adjectives in this verse?
- And what about those nouns [associated with verbs]?

This verb-based character or scene analysis will surely enhance the performance of the Drama style in terms of drama character development and performance guide. Moreover, as Florence suggests, when this verb-performative analysis is done with the congregants together (or at least with the worship drama team), the whole church's Dramatic Quotient (DQ)—I coined the term!—would greatly increase. This is discussed a bit further below in Practical Tips.

Practical Tips

- **Select Adoption of the Seven Traits:** The trait of **holistic artistry** prevails in the Drama style. The whole personality of the preacher would embody the Scriptural story, which is further magnified by various arts that accompany it. The trait of **fluidity** also works well in this style as the performed drama can interpret the Scriptural story from a fresh hermeneutical perspective (e.g., in the way of reader-response interpretation).[4] **Cross-cultural ubiquity** shows itself to have great potential as many different artistic images of biblical figures and symbols of Christ from various cultures may be easily adopted in this style. When the preacher happens to practice this style often, I encourage them to alternate different figures and symbols periodically, also adding new ones, so the sermon viewers develop a wide spectrum of multicultural perceptions of the biblical world.

- **Reading/Watching Literature and Media:** To perform the Drama style well, the preacher first should be able to write the sermon drama script well. And no, there is no easy quick path to becoming a fine drama script writer. The first rule of thumb is to read a good amount of literature (e.g., novels, poems, biographies, short nonfiction stories, etc.) and watch a variety of quality films, TV dramas, musicals, plays, or family recordings. Then, the second rule—probably more important and harder—is analyzing what is being read and watched. The habit of analysis is not easy at first as we tend to approach literature and media as entertainment and not as study materials. Yet, as the old saying goes, every piece of daily life can become an indispensable source of preaching life, and this is more so when it comes to the Drama style. Thus, the Drama style preacher, or preachers wanting to practice this style well from time to time, are recommended to develop a habit of reading/watching and analyzing literature and media. Once the habit is set in, the practice of analysis would be done unconsciously whenever reading and or watching. Analysis can be done on six narrative components: character, plot, setting, spectacle, music, and theme. Preachers should purchase a small paper journal or create an electronic Word or Excel chart on an electronic device such as a smartphone and carry it always; whenever opportunities arise to read, watch, and analyze, do so, and record them on the journal or the chart. Or, the preacher may want to designate an hour or two of the week solely for this threefold practice of reading, watching, and analyzing in a home office or somewhere else where no interruption happens. Either way, a steady habit of literature and media analysis would pay off hugely for the production of the Drama style of preaching.

An additional suggestion in this regard is to have a regular peer literature/media analysis group meeting. Already certain numbers of pastors around the nation host regular local lectionary group meetings. Why not use or add, from time to time, the same meeting for literary/media analysis? The collective wisdom of the group will be of great help and inspiration as different people interpret the same literature and media through various theological and cultural analytical lenses.

- Narrative Lectionary & Textweek.com: The Working Preacher website (https://www.workingpreacher.org) provides a free spin-off lectionary commentary program called the *Narrative Lectionary*. It is a church calendar-based four-year cycle of reading, consisting of the biblical stories from creation through the early Christian church (in other words, from Abraham and Sarah, Moses, and the prophets to Jesus and Paul). For a regular Drama style preacher needing consistent inspiration and different perspectives on stories, the Narrative Lectionary can be an invaluable source. It provides pastoral and expert commentaries on each story, along with a prayer of the day, hymn selections, and choral suggestions. It would be great to have regular Narrative Lectionary reflection meetings with the worship team members.

  The ever-popular Textweek.com could also be an amazing aid for the Drama style. This lectionary-based website literally provides a massive amount of literature and media resources for each week's readings. Those resources are not only good for the literature and media analysis practice, but also could serve as excellent sermon illustrations, brainstorming assistance, and supplemental liturgical elements (e.g., useful video clips played during the worship service or preaching). As a helpful tip, some weeks even provide drama resources for relevant texts that the Drama style preacher may want to make good use of.

- **Join a Local Theater Club:** To join a local theater club and play various roles, small or big, will certainly help the Drama style preacher's performative skills. Again, the preacher does not have to be a professional performer in order to deliver effective Drama preaching. Still, the preacher's diligent self-development in this regard would be a plus in many ways. If the preacher cannot join a local theater club for various reasons (one may be overwhelmed by local theatrical professionals), an alternative would be to start a friendly theater club in the church with the congregants. Together, they can read certain biblical stories based on Narrative Lectionary, write scripts collectively, and use props to perform them occasionally. Performances do not have to be full-scale ones that require plenty of preparation and stage materials. They can be done only verbally or with body movements in a small circle. This can also greatly improve the preacher's dramatic performative skills and the congregation's familiarity with a dramatization of biblical stories.

- **Collect Faith Artifacts:** Fine artifacts or props are essential for the Drama style. If the preacher can have a rich inventory of culturally diverse artifacts, it is a huge plus. This can't happen overnight. Thus, the preacher should collect items useful for the Drama production whenever there is an opportunity, and especially whenever the preacher travels to different parts of the nation or internationally. Simply be intentional in looking at market places or small shops and, if affordable, collecting diverse artifactual expressions of Christian faith that may later enrich the sermonic drama production. One will find there is practically no limit in the collecting effort, as ways of expressing faith are limitless. This could become the preacher's lifetime joy.

- **Sweet Ten-Minute Rule:** Practically speaking, the Drama style of preaching should run about ten minutes or so. Except for full-length movies, videos on YouTube these days are normally ten to twenty minutes in length. On TikTok, people do not even watch more than two or three minutes. Compared to high-tech video clips on YouTube or TikTok, the Drama sermon could be less attractive, at least in terms of graphic quality and digital editing. Yet again, we should recall Paul saying the "kingdom of God depends not on [spectacles] but on power" (1 Corinthians 4:20). We are not here to compete with tech-entertainment models, though we're very much open to learning necessary communicational tactics from them. That said, for the power of the Christian message to be truly impactful on the digital screen, it will do no harm to stick to the digital screen habit of the sermon viewers today. Let's keep the sweet ten-minute rule in mind.

Final Remarks

It would be nonsense or pretentious to say that there should be no fun or entertainment factor in the Drama style as it must be a solemn sermon. On the contrary, there *is*, if not *must be*, a fun and entertainment factor. After all, it is a drama, which is all about human life itself, which is full of joys, sorrow, triumphs, laughter, unexpected twists, sadness, fun, suffering, and smiles. Also, artifacts or props themselves will always create certain moments of natural humor. (Think of a puppet play.) Thus, there will always be "holy" fun in the Drama style.

But we should make sure that fun or entertainment is the not main drive for the sermon's meaning-making or the sermon viewer's interaction with preaching. The message or the inspiration of the message must be primary. Also, it is good to avoid any meaningless religious clichés or kitsch when selecting artifacts or props. (Of course, there is a lot of meaningful religious kitsch out there.) Each item must convey symbolism relevant to the biblical passage or the sermon message.

With all these concerns in mind, the Drama style certainly has great potential to be one of the most effective methods for online preaching. Who would not appreciate a fine Christian message that is both fun and serious?

Other Resources

Lajos Egri, *The Art of Dramatic Writing: Its Basis in the Creative Interpretation of Human Motives,* 1st ed. (New York: Simon & Schuster, 2004). Egri's classic is unique among the hundreds of how-to books in the market about drama script writing. This one deals with the fundamentals of script writing, including insights on character building that's based on basic human motives. Practical tips are provided as well.

Arland J. Hultgren, *The Parables of Jesus: A Commentary* (Grand Rapids, MI: Eerdmans, 2000). This volume provides in-depth theological and cultural insights into the (puzzling) parables of Jesus, thus is a useful resource on how to create sharp-witted dramas from the parables.

Notes

1 For example, see https://www.youtube.com/watch?v=8jab2CyCz6M& list=PLrDIc0LjcVUuI5q4n83NAX-OBGKxWBztm&index=100 (accessed October 10, 2020).

2 Mitchell Stephens, *The Rise of the Image, the Fall of the Word* (New York: Oxford University Press, 1998).

3 Anna Carter Florence, *Rehearsing Scripture: Discovering God's Word in Community* (Grand Rapids, MI: Eerdmans, 2018), 34–50.

4 Gerry Brenner, *Performative Criticism: Experiments in Reader Response* (Albany: State University of New York Press, 2004).Brenner argues for the performed text as a source of a fresh interpretation from the reader's vintage point of view.

CHAPTER 8

The Zoom/Chat Style

Figure 7[1]

General Description

This is a highly informal style of online preaching, at least in delivery, if not also in content. The preacher may even live Zoom-stream the message from a study or a quiet corner of a shopping mall. Note that Zoom is only one of many platforms these days; Facebook, YouTube, WeChat, and others have a similar live-stream function. The key is making the preaching environment as friendly and approachable as possible for listeners. Compared to the Podium style, which is the polar opposite, this style presents the preacher as a Christian on equal footing with the listener as they share their religious authority. The preacher "chats" with listeners as a good friend and hopes to address the concerns of daily life with great sympathy. This style gained popularity among preachers during the Covid-19 pandemic, thanks to its easy, low-tech usability for both the preacher and listeners. A great strength of this style is its ability to allow the preacher and listeners to have instant bilateral communication, either via the chat room or direct voice chatting. Churches, if their theology sanctions it, can even practice communion in this style because its technology allows people to simultaneously see each person's consumption of the elements.

Details of the Style

Who

The preacher is a kind of "next door" Uncle Joe or Auntie Susan. Once logged in, people immediately want to see a friendly smile and hear a greeting from the preacher. This friendship and hospitality originate from the primary functionality of Zoom or SNS mediums, specifically quick, amiable chats with friends, colleagues, or even strangers. Of course, these mediums have evolved to become formal communication platforms for workshops, business discussions, classroom lectures, and big conferences. But still, their original purpose as SNSs dominates; that is, light yet meaningful chats to whomever people would like to engage with.

Thus, a high expectation for the preacher from the sermon viewers is warm, congenial engagement with them before, during, and after the preaching event. In other words, not only *during* the sermon, but *before* and *after* it, people would be happy to chat with the preacher. Thus, it is recommended the preacher show up early, ten to fifteen minutes before worship begins, and remain on Zoom after the worship for a similar period for conversation with the interested sermon viewers. As a truly distinctive marker of Zoom preaching, in the mind of the people, the informal hangout would have almost the same (religious) significance as the formal hearing of the sermon. That is, chats are not merely small talks on small things of life, but their religious engagement with the preacher and spiritual commitment to the collective life of the church. Keeping all this in mind, therefore, the preacher should get actively involved in—seemingly so insignificant, but practically and spiritually so essential—chats before, during, and after the preaching.

Why

A huge economic advantage of the Zoom/Chat style cannot go unnoticed. The Zoom/Chat style is probably the least expensive option among all ten introduced in this book, thanks to its low-tech and minimum staffing requirements. The preacher alone can nearly do it all. Unlike the Interview style, the Metaverse style, the Drama style, and others which all need high-resolution cameras and professional tech staff, the preacher only needs a single laptop or desktop computer to fully practice the given style. That is exactly why during the Covid-19 pandemic, this style was most popular, as everyone, including the preacher, was supposed to stay at home, far distanced from each other. Even as people start gathering in person these days, whenever there is a similar need—for instance, a special service for people who are hospitalized or who are home-bound—the Zoom/Chat style is very useful. Everyone simply needs an online-connected screen device. In sum, the Zoom/Chat style elevates accessibility to the event of Christian worship and preaching at an unprecedented level.

The Zoom/Chat style can also elevate instant mutual communication between the preacher and sermon viewers by what I want to call homiletical chatting. As discussed more in *What* and Practical Tips below, the sermon viewers can communicate what they have in mind regarding the sermon or the focal text instantly (not waiting until the worship service ends) and can expect the preacher's immediate answers, even right in the middle of the sermon. And this activity of instant mutual questioning and answering is not simple, time-killing small talk, but *is* the significant homiletical practice of the sermon's meaning-making. In short, the sermon becomes whole and highly meaningful to both the preacher and the sermon viewers through the chats. In that respect, we could even state that in the Zoom/Chat style, the sermon is made and achieved *only* by actively involved homiletical chatting.

Where

The Zoom/Chat style, along with the Film/Vidpod style, provides full freedom in the practice of preaching. Technically, there is no limit to choosing a preaching place. Zoom even provides a Virtual Background function, via which preachers can hide where they are actually located. Of course, like the VR style, the virtual background does not look natural—though very realistic; still, it feels artificial, so there will be sermon viewers who may prefer real backgrounds such as the church office or the living room of a house. It is always good at the beginning for preachers to make a quick remark about where they are preaching from—including whether they are using a virtual background—so that the sermon viewers do not have too much curiosity about the place.

With hot spot Wi-Fi available, such other unconventional places as coffee shops, shopping malls, parks, marketplaces, street corners, furniture shops, wedding venues, and the like may go well with the Zoom/Chat style, as long as the given day's sermon text, the sermon topic, and the place match well. For instance, when preaching on the text around Jesus's Cana wedding visit in

John 2, why not go to an actual wedding service, set up a preaching booth, and preach from there? (With permission, of course!) The Cana wedding must have been "rowdy"; thus, it should be appropriate to preach in a similar rowdy place. As another instance, when preaching on Psalm 23, the preacher may want to set up a preaching pulpit in a natural park where green pasture is found, or at least in a grassy backyard of the church.

Relevant concerns around other liturgical elements (e.g., praise and worship or the choir) in relation to the preaching place are discussed in *When* and Practical Tips below.

When

Live sermon delivery is best for the Zoom/Chat style, which will enable instant chat communication between the preacher and the sermon viewers, as well as (if allowed) among the sermon viewers. While the sermon is live streamed, however, other liturgical components could be broadcast through prerecording. The reason is simple. Coordination of other live liturgical components carried out by other individuals located in different places does not flow smoothly in most cases. For instance, if the church has a choir or a praise and worship band, unless their members are in one place, performing live music on Zoom is difficult to do. Simpler orders as welcome, prayer, or announcements may work as live streaming. But again, doing the whole service as live streaming is not recommended for the reason of technical difficulties and in order to minimize people's confused attention.

The sermon does not *have* to be done through live streaming. Prerecorded preaching, like other worship orders, is a possibility. How will it go? In this scenario, preachers prerecord the sermon and then broadcast that recording live on Zoom. Then, preachers can have free-flowing chats with the sermon viewers while listening to the sermon with them—that is, preachers watching and having comments on their own sermon too! This highly collaborative practice of sermon deliberation may sound strange to most conventional preachers. But this is a unique techno-homiletical beauty and advantage of the Zoom/Chat style. Through this practice, the preaching event can become an adventurous communal and active democratic exercise; namely, anyone can participate in the communal liberative chat. It is quite adventurous because the preacher must be fully open to any—constructive or constructively deconstructive—live comments from the sermon viewers. The preacher may get different healthy interpretive perspectives on the Bible text and the sermon content. And vice versa, the sermon viewers may get fresh insights or challenges from the preacher that do not necessarily appear in the sermon itself. Altogether, the preacher and the sermon viewers might even develop totally different meanings on the given day's Bible passage. And why not? As preachers know well, one short sermon can't ever cover all the potential or hidden meanings of a single text. The preacher and the sermon viewers may be able to discuss many of them before, during, and after the preaching event. So, for Zoom preachers, it is recommended to do this prerecording and live deliberation practice occasionally for a good interpretive "shock" (again, the preacher may get totally different insights on the Bible passage, from chitchat to lay "theologians") and people's active democratic involvement in the sermon's meaning-making.

What

Preaching must be *bilateral chatting*. In this style, the preacher and the sermon viewers must make the sermon together through diligent dialogical interactions; that is, the sermon becomes whole only through those interactions, by either text chat or actual speaking (or both). This collaborative sermon-making, of course, must not release the preacher from a hard study of biblical passages. The best homiletical effectiveness of this style will surely depend on the preacher's deep knowledge and reflection on the passages from which the initial content of the sermon is born. Still, the preacher is the preacher. People will naturally expect more—more insights and simply even more speaking—from the preacher. Thus, the preacher should study and get ready for any questions or comments from the sermon viewers.

Since the sermon viewers' participation in the making of the sermon is key to the Zoom/Chat style's effectiveness, it is always better for the preacher's share of the sermon to be highly open-ended. The preacher prepares and brings something to the table, based on which *bilateral chatting* will flow. That something must be both substantial and open-ended; substantial enough to spark the people's deep thoughts and reflection on the day's passage and topic, and then open-ended enough to make room for the people's own interpretation of the passage and their critical engagement with the topic. Depending on the preacher's prehomiletical design, the contribution ratio to the sermon-making between the preacher and the sermon viewers could be 50:50, 70:30, or even 30:70, meaning that the sermon viewers might contribute more to the sermon-making than the preacher. This certainly does not mean the preacher is lazy or not "smart enough," but rather should mean the sermon is inspirational enough to draw the people's enthusiastic engagement with the sermon. In short, for the Zoom/Chat-style, like all other styles, the preacher's hard-thought-out planning is greatly important for the style's communication appeal to the sermon viewers and its homiletical fruitfulness.

Useful Homiletic Theory

The Zoom/Chat style is a recent and unconventional development, so no readily relevant homiletic theory is found on the market for this style. That said, there are at least one or two homiletical methods that could assist the Zoom/Chat-style preacher to effectively "chat" during sermon delivery with congregants.

Wilson's *The Four Pages of the Sermon* mentioned in Chapter One comes as the first.[2] This four-stage movement of the sermon can be highly useful and functional for the Zoom preacher, especially when generating active interactional chats between the preacher and the sermon participants. For instance, through Page One the preacher might want to explore life's problems appearing in the biblical world and stop there for a while for back-and-forth questions and answers with the congregation. The preacher may ask, "What problems do you see? How do you feel about those problems or the sins? Do we see anything like that in our world too?" Then, through Page Two, the preacher might explore in depth similar problems in our world. Then, again stop there for a while, asking (or chatting), "Why do you think similar problems still continue in our world since biblical times? Do you think they are really similar or somewhat different? In what ways?" Now through Page Three and Four, the preacher could move on to the grace of God or fine resolutions appearing in the biblical world and that of today with a similar back-and-forth questioning and answering pattern. As one can easily imagine, this pattern will generate active and engaging chats among all the participants. As a prolonged variation, the preacher may want to have six or eight Pages, repeating each Page or even covering the four-page process twice for a deeper understanding of the sin and the grace of God showing up in the biblical world and today's context.

Verse-by-verse preaching is another homiletical method that could work very well. Traditionally, this method is used by the preacher when they want to expound every single verse in depth, though also, of course, in connection with other verses. Typically, the preacher's communication is unilateral. However, Zoom preachers can also make use of this method, transforming its unilateral communication to bilateral. The method is simple, yet profound; preachers can expound each verse as in the traditional way, and then stop for a while for interpretive chatting with the sermon participants, asking, for instance, "What do you think about my quick exploration of the first verse? Do you agree with my thoughts? What more can be done interpretively on this verse?" Again, with this simple tweaking of verse-by-verse preaching, the preacher should be able to increase the people's engagement level of homiletical chatting.

Practical Tips

- **Select Adoption of the Seven Traits:** The two traits of **instant communication** and **shareability** are prominent in this style. Regarding instant communication before, during, and after sermon delivery, listeners or viewers[3] can initiate questions or comments about the sermon. For instance, during the sermon, a viewer may post a question in the chat room about a theological concept introduced by the preacher to elicit further conversation. The preacher, noticing the question feed, may choose to immediately engage the question. The reverse may also happen.

During the sermon, the preacher may ask a question of viewers and they may immediately post their answers in the chat room or answer the question through live talking. Whereas we may have thought that "preaching is fulfilled in the hearing of the listener" (Fred B. Craddock), this style of preaching in the present digital age suggests that "preaching is fulfilled in the midst of the sermonic dialogue."

The Zoom/Chat style lends itself to hypershareability with other social media outlets like YouTube and Facebook. The live sermon occurring on Zoom can be also simultaneously broadcasted on YouTube and Facebook. This helps the sermon to be shared virtually worldwide by only a simple click on a hyperlink. As a result, a very high level of connectivity of the revealed Word is achievable, especially during times of virtual communion, when people can connect with each other in the same body of Christ in one virtual place, wherever they may reside physically, be it Africa, Asia, Europe, South America, or anywhere else.

- **Fifteen Minutes Before; Thirty Minutes After:** As mentioned, live chats with the sermon audience before, during, and after the sermon are important in the effective execution of the Zoom/Chat style. The question then is, how long? The preacher certainly can't be with the people for an hour before or after the service, but neither can the time be too short (say, five minutes). An appropriate length depends on each context, but quality time should still be guaranteed.

The author's multiple field experiences show that fifteen minutes before the service and thirty minutes after the service seems to work well. Before the service, people may engage in lighter chats, including weather or last week's sermon, while after the service, people might want to have lively, serious chats on the day's message. The preacher does not have to stay the whole time or when extra time is needed (which is, most times, a good sign!). The preacher may ask a lay leader of the congregation to continue the after-service chats. Whether it is the preacher or a lay leader, the important thing is having a high-quality sermonic chat experience. Preachers, from time to time, may want to have a thorough reflective analysis of their own chat practice.

- **Rules or No Rules?:** In the Zoom/Chat style, anyone can participate in the chat, verbally or by text. Anyone can include total strangers. In one sense, this is not a problem at all. The church—as a gathering place of all people—can or should welcome newcomers who are totally unknown. Yet due to the heightened level of anonymity in the digital space and meeting total strangers, this may pose a caveat. Thus, some churches screen who can enter the Zoom space; either worshippers should be a registered member or contact the church office before the worship service begins. Ideally (I admit!), the church's worship space should be open to anyone who wants to be in the worship service. Thus, a good compromise will be a real-time screening of people's behavior and language use. As the Zoom/Chat style expects free, lively, and meaningful chats, any attempts to prevent them should be immediately sanctioned, which is possible through Zoom's useful functions like Mute or Remove. It'd be better for a church staffer or lay leader, rather than the preacher, to take this moderator role. Also, each time when Zoom is on, it is helpful to share the church's short list of rules for Zoom chatting so that all participants will have a common ground for digital engagement.

- **Dos and Don'ts:** Chatting happens in the context of worship. Thus, there is a certain expectation of what to say and what not to say. Listing what to say and what not to say is a useful guide both for the preacher and sermon chatters (again, my own terminology!). Here is a list, though it is by no means exhaustive:

What to Say

⇒ Chats on weather
⇒ Welcoming newcomers and faces that haven't been seen in a while
⇒ Ask each other's whereabouts
⇒ Ask each other's recent faith journey
⇒ Comment on last week's and this week's sermons
⇒ Comment on this week's overall worship
⇒ Encourage people to share good news in life, if any, in a moderate sense (see below)—for example, mom's birthday, wedding anniversary, college graduation, running 5K successfully, learning cooking, or watching a fine musical

⇒ Compliment on other's good works during the given week, if known

⇒ Share any good news of the church

⇒ The preacher's blessings when closing each chat before or after the service

What Not to Say

⇒ Do not ask specifically about personal struggles or hardships unless people voluntarily want to share about them or unless those come up naturally during the conversation; rather, ask if people have any prayer concerns

⇒ Things that the preacher only knows about certain people (don't ask their permissions to talk about those on the spot)

⇒ Any comments on people's personal appearances

⇒ The church's financial situation

⇒ One's excessive success stories in business or something else

⇒ Gossip about congregants or public figures

⇒ Specific political views or opinions

⇒ Church event announcements

⇒ The preacher's personal life

⇒ Another minisermon (by the preacher!)

Obviously, the preacher or the chat moderator takes an important role in "regulating" people's chats, especially regarding *What Not to Say*. It's recommended that a church develop its own practical protocols on the chat regulation that can be announced

or posted somewhere visible on the church's website, or this can be posted in the chat room as a cordial reminder for all participants each time when
the chat begins.

- **Questions, Questions, Questions:** It's always good for the
preacher to prepare (new) sets of questions each
time as chat starters, questions on welcome, reflective questions on the previous sermon (e.g., "Do you
have any lingering reflection over last week's sermon?
Any new thoughts came up throughout the week?"),
and thought-raising questions on the day's sermon.
It is good to have differently nuanced questions each
time. It is natural for the participants to become
uninterested if the preacher makes use of the same
sets of questions over and over again. Questions
based on *What to Say* are desirable starting points.

Final Remarks

Get ready to engage, actively and sincerely. The preacher must
actively engage in chats before, during, and after the worship
service/sermon. This practice is not familiar to most conventional preachers, admittedly. We are good at the church thresh-
old goodbye greetings or coffee hour chats, but certainly not at
chats—both fun and serious—around the sermon. Yet, think
of Jesus, the master preacher, who was mostly on the streets for
proclamation. According to the Gospels, his engagement is natural and active. People often talk back to him, and he does not
hesitate to engage. It is done completely in public, and there is
no hiding place. And many times, his engagement seems to be

highly effective in terms of raising people's critical religious consciousness and provoking new ways of life. Free talk works, even on religious matters!

We now have a digital public space for similar sermonic engagement, though specific methods are different (e.g., text chatting). Like Jesus, this open public space can be both a great opportunity and a risk. It is a risk in the sense that the preacher may not immediately have good answers to people's random questions. But at the same time, it is an opportunity to directly hear from sermon participants about their critical, healthy thoughts on the sermon, and also, perhaps more importantly, about their daily lives. These days some folks feel more comfortable sharing their life concerns, joys, and prayer requests online rather than in person. Thus, Zoom chatting could be a fine form of pastoral care today, beyond talks and discussions on sermons. So, why not?

Other Resources

Ronald J. Allen, *Patterns of Preaching: A Sermon Sampler* (St. Louis, MO: Chalice Press, 1998).
As mentioned, currently there is no applicable homiletical theories to the Zoom/Chat style in the market. Yet, the preacher may want to make good use of various existing theories of preaching on Zoom as we have experimented with above. This volume introduces existing theories of preaching in a concise manner with fine sermon samplers.
O. Wesley Allen Jr., *Determining the Form: Structures for Preaching* (Minneapolis, MN: Fortress Press, 2008).
The readers can find additional useful sermon forms in this volume, including quick, applicable introductions to the Four Pages form and the verse-by-verse form.

Notes

1 "8-30-2020 Service.Mp4," Google Docs, accessed October 10, 2020, https://drive.google.com/file/d/1sN57LIyaLaC8MqR-mrQRdeMfPdil0W8M/view?usp=sharing.

2 Wilson, *The Four Pages of the Sermon: A Guide to Biblical Preaching.*

3 With regard to online preaching, the traditional designation of "listener" does not seem to reflect the online communicative reality. Rather, the concept of "viewer" may better serve as listeners now hear and watch *on the screen*, like watching a film, not only the preacher but also other holistic artistic elements.

CHAPTER 9

The Rock Concert Style

Figure 8[1]

General Description

Preachers of the Rock Concert (RC) style often roam around the worship "stage." The preacher may begin the sermon from the podium with the Bible on it; then, as the sermon develops to its climax, the preacher may engage the listeners more energetically by approaching them closely or by the embodied performance of the preached Word. At times, especially when using dramatic shout-outs or high pitches, the praise band will accompany the preacher for a synergistic effect, generating the feel of a live rock concert. Listeners or worship-goers, like concert-goers, participate in the sermonic concert by shouting back, humming, laughing out loud, or clapping. They actively respond to the preaching event, even to the point of *completing* the sermon through their contributions. Indeed, without their contributions, the preacher's performance and delivery would fail in their effectiveness.

In Figure 8, active worship participants are still portrayed (as in times prior to the pandemic), but in actual online preaching they are not present.[2] This portrayal is intentional because the preacher of the RC style still strives to create a concert-like feel for online preaching while having only a minimal, yet fully operative, worship staff. A smaller music band will accompany the preacher while a minimum amount of church staff will play the role of worship-goers.

Details of the Style

Who

The preacher is a humble yet highly performative presenter of the gospel. Yes, worship-goers would like to see both wholehearted humility and genuine Spirit-led performance from the preacher. Humility, at times, might get overshadowed by the preacher's dynamic performance, which the preacher sooner or later should correct during the sermon through reinstated humility interwoven in the message and performance.

As an RC-style gospel performer, the preacher is expected to be an enthusiastic and interactive communicator. The preacher should be capable of doing joyful shouting (of course, not all the time!), presenting a highly visible performance, uplifting the people's emotions, and also "instigating" listeners' bodily and verbal expressions—such as clapping or saying, "Preach," "Yeah," or "Amen"—as their lively responses to the gospel message. The bottom line is, the preacher must interact with church-goers. While some styles of preaching are performative without avid interaction, this isn't the case for RC-style preaching.

As a highly performative style, there is a danger that the RC preacher's unfiltered ego might get in the way of presenting and hearing the gospel. At the same time, however, the RC style, when adopted prudently, can be an exciting tool for interactional online preaching. Excitement about the gospel and spirited interaction are important traits of all online preaching, as online worshippers can get distracted easily. No doubt then, there is a good raison d'être for the RC style.

Why

First off, some preachers are born with an innate performative character. The best way they can communicate messages is through full energetic embodiment in public speaking. They need to walk around, make various facial expressions, move hands in multiple directions, and at times, speak directly to the audience to make points. They can't make good speeches unless there are considerate verbal responses from the live audience. This back-and-forth communicative practice (or in the Black tradition, the call-and-response practice) truly animates RC-style preaching. All this said, however, other preachers unfamiliar with the RC style surely can practice the RC style with some basic training. More on this will be discussed later in Practical Tips.

The RC style is good for the attention-grabbing effect it has on sermon viewers. It is now common knowledge that the attention span of most digital sermon viewers is *very short*. Plus, in general, it is a "miracle" if digital consumer-viewers can bear more than ten to twenty minutes watching the same content before turning to different shows or channels, unless the content is like those of well-plotted dramas, exciting movies, or big sports events (all these being highly visual and aural). When it comes to online preaching, most of which is done as only a verbal event, consumer-viewer attitudes can be challenging. The RC style provides an appropriate approach to that problem. Through the preacher's bodily performance, the band's accompanying music, and the staff's back-and-forth response/ shouting, the RC style creates a sacred show, drama, and/or performance that can appeal to today's multisensory hearing and viewing-favoring sermon participants.

Where

An elevated worship stage looking like an indoor concert hall works best for the RC style. The stage should be large enough to arrange the worship band, the podium (rather than the pulpit), various artistic installments, lights, other temporary stage decorations, and the like. All this means is that conventional pulpit- or table-centered sanctuary-type worship places would not work for RC-style preaching. Instead, modern worship spaces built for seekers or praise-and-worship-type services would work better. Truth be told, in most cases, RC-style preachers design and build stage-type worship spaces for their new church buildings.

As Figure 8 shows, the preacher is not alone on the worship stage but rather is surrounded by the worship band and a small group of church staff. For online preaching, the band and the church staff are "real" worship participants in the sense that they are the ones who perform the back-and-forth interactional shouting with the preacher. Again, without their energetic participation, the preaching is only half complete; the preacher would lose focus and passion. Their accompanying music (the drum roll!) and passionate verbal affirmation of preaching will make the preaching whole.

At times, the performative preacher will have useful props or installation arts to enhance the performed message, which are mostly placed on the stage. A rule of thumb is that those items, by their glitz or exotic appearances, must not overshadow the preacher or the message. Principally, their raison d'être is to augment the performative feature of preaching. For that purpose, the preacher is expected to communicate and plan with the worship arts team very closely weeks before.

When

Live streaming is best. Typically, it makes a huge positive difference for performative preachers when they know there is a real-time audience: "The people are with me *right now* (and *here* online), so I need to work hard to get connected with them." This is why it is great to let performative preachers see as many faces of worship participants as possible on a big screen installed in front of them. Then, the preachers will know people are out there *with them*, sincerely performing God's Word.

It won't be helpful to allow live online sermon viewers to actually say something in the back-and-forth style; there is always a risk that two or three people may say things at the same time and the central audio sound gets muffled instantly and easily. It will be the job of the worship band and the church staff on the stage to verbally interact with the preacher. Sermon viewers can still make fine performative contributions by using emoji and text chats, which can appear on the same big screen. The preacher, no doubt, would be greatly energized seeing the live sermon viewers' passionate interaction with the sermonic performance. Who wouldn't?

Prerecording is possible too, but less successful in terms of the sermon viewers' active participation in the preaching event. In this case, the role of the worship band and the church staff in making the sermon event whole and elevated will take on more importance. That is, the worship band and the church staff should function homiletical interactionally very well (i.e., the back-and-forth dynamic) so that the preacher does not lose the sense of liveliness.

What

As in Zoom/Chat style-preaching, RC-style preaching must be *bilateral* in its fundamental ecclesial nature. The preacher must be in good sync with the worship band, the church staff, and the live audience. Yet unlike the Zoom sermon, which is highly bilateral in sermon delivery, even to the extent that the sermon content could change significantly, the RC preacher may sound like a confident herald or a performative priest bringing the entirety of the sacred Word to the audience. That is, the preacher will have the entire desired sermon content in hand. Even so, the spirit of the sermon, which may have equal weight to the sermon content for the RC style when it comes to effective communication, cannot be complete without the live audience's impassioned engagement. Plus, at times, just like in the Zoom preaching, the preacher may improvise on the planned sermon as the audience's engagement (see *Who*) needs it. This would not be the norm but is still possible.

As part of a sermonic performance, poetic, metaphorical, or symbolic wording will make its appearance often. This performative-poetic wording will go hand in hand with the performative interpretation of the biblical passage. In other words, the preacher is not performing because the preacher simply likes doing it or wants to make the sermon more entertaining, but because the performative interpretation and embodiment of the biblical passage expects it. More is discussed below in Useful Homiletic Theory.

Useful Homiletic Theory

There is no better source in the market for the interactional consideration between preaching and performance than Jana Childers's *Performing the Word: Preaching as Theatre*.[3] Childers proposes "a lively homiletic" for the theoretical naming of performance-based preaching. She realizes that all preaching has a performative nature and should be lively. What she does in the volume is 1) a 360-degree thorough analysis of preaching as performance and 2) a presentation of useful lessons from theater studies for the pulpit performance, which is unprecedented. There are many takeaways from the volume, but for RC- style preaching, the following three are of great importance.

First, the performance of the text itself *is* textual interpretation. Thus, performative preaching in its truest sense begins with the performed text, not with the sermon script written for performance. When it comes to the textual interpretation, "it is the job of the preacher to sniff out the shape of the text, to see where it peaks and what devices it uses to build momentum to reach that point. Obviously, it is also the preacher who decides which part of her or his face and body will carry forward the life of the text."[4] All these performative-interpretive dimensions will appear in the actual delivery of the sermon.

Second, keep in mind the performative performer's threefold habitus. Habitus #1 is a commitment to energy. The actor—and thus the performative preacher—should strive to bring life (or presence, vitality, or projection) to the stage. This certainly does not mean that the preacher always must shout out, cry out, yell, or move around busily. No. Vitality can be achieved by sheer silence too. The point is the purposeful or well-planned performative projection of the preacher's emotions and thoughts,

whether through purposeful silence or energetic action. Habitus #2 is a respect for the body, which can mean two things.
First, avoid both unintentional bodily mannerisms and excess
movement. Mannerisms happen when performative preachers
do not give careful attention to details of their body movements,
while excess movements can happen when preachers attempt to
hide their lack of sermon preparation through overexaggerated
motions. There is a good chance that both may hinder the congregation from focusing on the scriptural message itself. "The
goal is to create of the body a kind of clean slate—if not a tabula
rasa—on which the text... can express itself."[5] Second, project a
healthy view of the body and cultivate a good habit of keeping
it in a fine fit and available for any necessary sermonic action, in
accordance with each preacher's unique kinetic circumstances.
Preachers of all shapes, sizes, and physical abilities may use this
style effectively; embodied presence is the key. Historically, in
some Christian circles, we have regarded flesh as evil and, thus,
relegated its cultivation to the side. The RC-style preaching provides a sacred venue to overcome that misguided perception of
the human body. Now habitus #3, as the most general and fundamental rule, is that the performative preacher should create a
space of hospitality. The preacher's performance should be never
intended for the preacher's own self-obsessed or self-satisfying
cathartic moments, which unfortunately can happen. No. The
performance should be the clean slate or window through which
the congregation is warmly invited into the biblical salvific
drama so that they can find and act out their own roles in that
drama. The performative preacher must be a kind, informed,
and hospitable guide of the people for that purpose.

Third, perceive the entire worship as theater. It is always
good for the preacher's sermonic performance to be interwoven

with the rest of the dramatic worship—not in the sense of sudden emotional twists, but in the sense of God's salvific drama. In other words, the whole worship can be a theo-theatrical presentation (more on this in Practical Tips), of which performative preaching is a significant part. Then, the congregation would not see the sermonic performance as a solely dramatized piece apart from the rest of worship, but as a performative-thematic continuation of the whole.

In sum, it is very important for the RC style's highly performative nature that a preacher must be conscious of physical movement so that it can be a fine-tuned, hospitable conduit of the scriptural message. Undoubtedly, the people would be pleased and touched by God's salvific drama performed enthusiastically yet with humility by the faithful RC preacher—the preacher not as a rock star, but a starry servant of the Word.

Practical Tips

- **Select Adoption of the Seven Traits:** The two traits of **fluidity** and **holistic artistry** thrive in this style. The musically performed Word by the preacher opens the way for creative interpretations of the Word; that is, the same Word can be performed differently as an interpretive act both by the preacher and worship participants at different times. (As noted above, in this style, worshippers can also participate in the sermon event by their own affirmative verbal actions.) Strictly speaking, no two performances acted out at different times are ever the same. That being the case, the performed Word often opens the positive floodgate for unbounded or fluid hermeneutical possibilities of the Word proclaimed. After all, the performed Word is holistic-artistic. Since no piece of art invites just one fixed interpretation of itself, it invites ongoing interpretation.

- **Worship as Theo-theater:** It is always good for any worship service to be coherent in its entirety: thematically, musically, theologically, performatively, and all other possible ways. Worship in which RC-style preaching occurs is no exception. Coherence is of great significance for RC-style preaching, as there is a good chance that the preaching performance may stick out to the extent that it gets all the liturgical prominence, which must not be so for any fine worship service. Designing the whole worship as a theo-theatrical drama of which the preaching performance is one part is a fine resolution for the issue. Worship as a theo-theatrical drama, briefly defined, can mean worship having a theatrical narrative arc and relevant performance pieces (e.g., acting, dancing, music, reading, and decoration). Admittedly, there are notable limitations in designing the online service in a theatrical sense, but still, there are practical suggestions for it as follows:

  ○ Design worship through a narrative arc; namely, setup, conflict/problems, climax/resolution, and ending. For instance, 1) the opening song(s) might serve as setup, 2) prayer after the singing would narrate the problems of the world in light of the sermon passage for the day, 3) the RC- style preaching presents and performs the climax and resolution of the problems, and 4) the sermon ends with blessings.

- Decorate the worship stage with items or props relevant to the biblical text or the sermon's topic.
- Play short video clips when available from biblical films or TV dramas in connection with the sermon.
- Dramatic reading of Scripture always helps.
- Liturgical or worship dancing will be of great help, adding performative dynamics to the worship band's singing.
- Play music videos produced by the church staff or the worship band. They can lessen the burdens of staging live worship dancing.
- Ask the sermon viewers to prepare their own props that they can show on the big screen to the preacher during the sermon, as a virtual interactional activity. For this, the preacher may want to make a pre-worship announcement about the upcoming sermon's topic and its associated biblical passage.

- **Pitch Rhetorical Questions:** The performative preacher's passionate actions may not be enough to arouse the responsive actions of the digital screen-viewing congregants. Instead, we may find silence, if not ignorance. (Have we all not been there?) Then, rhetorical questions, coupled with the preacher's interpretive performance, will help. Good sermonic questions always make people think and engage. Rhetorical questions in this case are the ones that people do not need to answer, but that they are "compelled" to respond to with such exclamation voices as "Yes, Lord," "Right, preach," "Oh, no...," "Surely," and "Amen!" Just imagine any fine Rock n' Roll concert hall. What do people do? As the band sings, the people scream (in an utter trance!), shout out, dance around, raise their hands, sing along, and even prostrate, which all can be summed up as *responsive reactions* to something they feel passionate about. Here is a lesson. Pitch performative-rhetorical questions around things that people deeply care about. Then, the people will return their responsive verbal or emoji performance to the preacher's compelling words—that is, ultimately to the Word coming from above.

- **Aspiring or Seasoned:** Let's admit it; the RC style is not for everyone. It requires specific performative sensitivity and training. With that said, however, the RC style is not beyond any preacher's potential or capacity. The thing is that, to exaggerate, there can be no fine preaching without fine performance. Preachers know by instinct or practice that they always perform. In that sense, the RC style is only an intentional stretch of what the preachers already do. Hence, both aspiring and seasoned preachers who are not familiar with the RC style can try this attractive preaching method with some good intentions and training. Even the training can be convenient: 1) Simply watch some fine RC preachers on

YouTube or their church websites. 2) Analyze and take notes on their use of verbal and body language, as well as their interaction with the sermon viewers. 3) Go back to one of your recent or old sermon scripts. 4) Revise the script following your notes. 5) Practice your own RC sermon in front of the mirror in the living room. This simple five-step exercise when done repeatedly for a certain period (say six months) can make a significant change in one's RC style. This can be an exciting journey of new homiletical learning.

- **Interpretive Reviews and Replies:** Ask the sermon viewers to leave reviews of the sermon on the church's website or on the app where the sermon clip is posted as they typically and happily do on Google, Rotten Tomatoes, and other web platforms for the movies, TV shows and theater plays they watch daily. The preacher doesn't have to respond to them all, though they may want to do so. The point is not a critical review of the preacher's acting performance per se, but the reviewers' original interpretive thoughts on the preacher's textual performance. Now that the preacher has provided a personal performative interpretation of the given passage, the reviewers may want to present their own from their own artistic perspectives. The performed Word is holistic-artistic. No piece of art can claim only one fixed interpretation of the subject, object, or text that it creatively presents; rather, it invites ongoing interpretation. Thus, how about practicing the same for the RC style of performative-artistic preaching? The reviewers' thoughts on the performed Word would truly enrich the breadth, width, and depth of the textual-performative enterprise initiated by the preacher but continued sincerely by a multitude of God's holy people.

Final Remarks

Entertainment, or performative entertainment, aspects cannot be ignored in the RC style. They are simply there, to be frank. (In any circumstances and all kinds of preaching, what the preacher does is the *performed* Word. Isn't that right?). Also, let's not forget that all online preaching is streamed or recorded by digital cameras and appears on services like YouTube, Zoom, Facebook, and TikTok to be watched through digital screens of smartphones, tablets, laptops, or other screens. All these digital gadgets and apps were never originally meant for religious use, not to mention preaching. They were all invented for either digitized communication, work, or entertainment. Online preaching happens to make good use of them. Thus, in a critical sense, with these entertaining digital gadgets adopted, it is mere nonsense to say that online preaching is purely free from any entertainment ethos and content. *They are simply there.* Thus, it is also absurd to say that, due to the entertainment aspects, we must shy away from RC- style preaching. It would be a classic case of throwing the baby out with the bathwater. What should be considered instead is how to render the performance of the Word more gospel-oriented and Christ-centered, rather than entertainment-driven. This can only be done by the diligence of the preacher. The task is not easy (who said preaching would be easy?), but the end result is so fruitful both for the preacher and the sermon viewers. During the pandemic, many good RC preachers have proved it!

Other Resources

Jana Childers and Clayton J. Schmit, *Performance in Preaching: Bringing the Sermon to Life*, Engaging Worship (Grand Rapids, MI: Baker Academic, 2008).

This volume, though largely academic, is an excellent source for any preachers interested in the in-depth exploration of the hermeneutical intersection between preaching and performance. The companion DVD provides useful practical suggestions for performative preaching.

Richard F. Ward, *Speaking from the Heart: Preaching with Passion* (Nashville, TN: Abingdon Press, 1992).

Ward, with a practical homiletical sense, helps preachers develop a healthy habit of preparing and delivering genuinely compassionate preaching. Chapter 6, "The Listener as Active Participant," is so insightful for RC- style preaching.

Notes

1 "When Anxiety Attacks | Pastor Steven Furtick | Elevation Church," October 17, 2016, accessed October 10, 2020, https://www.youtube.com/watch?v=dMpzvw4yhB8&feature=emb_title.

2 "When They Found Out | Pastor Steven Furtick | Elevation Church," September 14, 2020, accessed October 10, 2022, https://www.youtube.com/watch?v=lW916Mcl1Ow&feature=emb_title.

3 Jana Childers, *Performing the Word: Preaching as Theatre* (Nashville, TN: Abingdon Press, 1998).

4 Childers, *Performing the Word: Preaching as Theatre*, 79.

5 Childers, *Performing the Word: Preaching as Theatre*, 115.

CHAPTER 10

The Film/Vidpod Style[1]

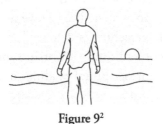

Figure 9[2]

General Description

The Film/Vidpod style, a cutting-edge sermonic production of the digital media age, is rapidly emerging as an avant-garde alternative to conventional preaching. It is unconventional in several ways: preaching does not happen in a church building (filmed shots of the sermon can happen anywhere around the world); preachers do not actually appear in the sermonic film, but sermon viewers only listen to their voice; music—including various songs or a variety of instrumental music—often accompanies the sermon from beginning to end; in all cases, preaching is prerecorded with a preacher's voice added to filmed shorts and can be streamed any time, any day; several preachers can preach a sermon together by their coordinated narrations or each preacher can take turns on different Sundays; and finally, preachers do not have to live near the church or their congregation but can be located anywhere, just like the viewers. Thus, the figure standing in Figure 9 is actually not the preacher. The figure is a performer in this sermonic film whose performance relates to the Scripture reading and the sermon's subthemes. In fact, the sermonic film moves from scene to scene and changes its performers in accordance with the subthematic movements of the sermon. Music will also constantly change to match these movements. Typically, the Film/Vidpod-style preaching is delivered in a stand-alone format, without any other liturgy or worship components accompanying it except for Scriptural reading, opening prayer, and benediction at the end.

Details of the Style

Who

The preacher takes up a threefold homiletical role: sermonic scriptwriter, film director, and narrator. After study and reflection on scriptural passages, the preacher will write a sermonic film script, plan the filming (including purchasing relevant items, recruiting actors and a film crew, if necessary, decisions on locations, etc.), direct the filming (including voice narrating), and finally edit what is filmed and voice-added with the tech professional. Basically, the preacher is involved in nearly every single step of filming the sermon, which makes sense, as the preacher will want to have homiletical input on each important step. As discussed further in Practical Tips, it is even possible that the preacher can do it *all* without a professional film crew and digital editor, which definitely helps lower the production cost. Thankfully, many free and paid websites and apps are available for filming and editing.

The preacher's role goes beyond that of procedural and technical matters. The preacher must have a keen hermeneutical sense, "a hermeneutic of naming grace" in daily life.[3] To be clear, homiletical filming (the Vidpod, henceforth) is not like Hollywood blockbusters or avant-garde indie films produced for only a targeted group of people. The Vidpod aims to name God's grace abundant in everyday life, illuminated by Scriptural evidence and guidance, for the sake of general congregants seeking God's love and care in their own context. Thus, preachers could do this job well with continued faithful attempts to see and film God's footprints embedded within their and other people's lives. In that sense, the preacher's fourth role would be as a scripturally guided observer and commentator on daily human life. The preacher's profound task will be hermeneutically connecting the biblical world and the filmed world of today.

It is noteworthy that the Vidpod preacher can be an independent preacher, belonging formally to no church at all, as this style does not necessarily require any conventional pulpit. Preachers can have their own websites, or various SNS sites can be their "pulpit" and "church." As the old saying goes, the church is not a building where the people go, but *the people* wherever they may gather are the church. Thus, if people can "gather" around the preacher's website or SNS pages, that collective online presence could be considered a church gathering. This matter will be more discussed in Practical Tips later below.

Why

A wide and "wild" outreach is a strong ecclesial merit of this style. It is wide in the sense that in today's image-driven and entertainment-oriented world, moving image-based filmic preaching can have a great chance to reach the hearts of a great number of people for their good. (Did you know that the famous TED conference stands for technology, entertainment, and design? In this case "entertainment" does not seem to be associated with its typical—misguided—perception of "lightness" or "shallowness" at all!) This preaching style's outreach is wild, too, in the sense that any filmic sermon can be distributed to anyone and everyone on countless social media platforms with almost no restrictions—in a matter of a second, literally. Surely, all online preaching contents of other preaching styles explored in this book can be just as widely sharable as that of the Vidpod style. Yet a huge conceptual difference between the Vidpod and others regarding this matter is that the Vidpod presents sermonic content that sounds and looks like a well-made spiritual or inspirational film, not a sermon perceived in its conventionality (e.g., think quickly of the Podium style). Put bluntly, there is a better chance for people with short digital attention spans to quickly check out sermonic films rather than watch an actual clergy person's verbal communication. This is undeniably the Vidpod's greatest merit.

Homiletically speaking, the Vidpod style demonstrates a happy, total integration between words and moving images, along with music. Maybe would this be the centuries-old dream of the preacher finally coming true? Jesus was a fine integrator between words and images when uttering various types of real-life image-driven parables. Yet, people only *heard* of those images from Jesus; they could not actually see them in front of them. On one hand, this might be better in a pedagogical sense, since the hearers would begin their own imaginative process in their heads. But, as the old-time-proven saying goes, a picture is worth a thousand words. If the hearers can see what is being said readily, they can *get it*—intended inspirations or insights—immediately. The Vidpod style makes that possible. Who knows? Jesus might have used YouTube clips had he had them during his time—after all, he used many fine cultural images and stories people simply knew well, like those found on today's YouTube.

Where

The Vidpod style can be the most radical among all styles in this regard. There are no constraints when it comes to where preaching is done and how it is prepared. First, the filming can happen anywhere, be it a church, home, beach, coffee café, sports arena, mountain, plane, boat, kitchen, car, shopping mall, or even a secret closet! Simply unlimited possibilities. Then, when the preacher has to add speech and edit the filmed shots, it can also be done anywhere and everywhere with a laptop in hand. Wherever there is a quiet environment, that place will be a preacher's sanctuary. For special occasions, the preacher may want to choose a noisy place like a café on purpose. The purpose could be an unexpected *encounter of God's presence in mundane places*. With the noisy background, the preacher may actually show this.

These days, Vidpods can be made easily. There are numerous free or paid images, video clips, and sound files available online. This means that preachers do not really have to film shots by themselves at all. They are simply out there to be used and edited wisely. All the preacher must do is come up with a good sermon idea, use customizable resources faithfully in the preacher's own office, and then finally post it on the church's website or a variety of social media platforms. In short, from preparation to actual delivery of the sermon, the preacher does not have to make a single visit to the brick-and-mortar church, which is not strange for the Vidpod style at all.

When

Live streaming is not an option for the Vidpod style as its preaching is always prerecorded. Thanks to its prerecording, preaching then can be posted any time and any day throughout the week; Sunday morning sounds like one of seven options. Yet it is important to remember that in the church's life or one's faith practice, ritualistic rhythm is significant. In other words, the habit of practicing the same liturgical ritual at a designated time of the week is essential in one's week-based faith development. (After all, Christians have kept Sunday as the Lord's Day for the past two millennia and will probably keep doing so for another millennium!) Thus, it would be better to post the prerecorded sermon on a designated day of the week, and probably the best day for it would be Sunday, again, as a majority of Christians are used to observing Sunday as the Sabbath. Otherwise, people's ritualistic rhythm would get muddled, and eventually, there is a chance that watching online preaching would become an occasional event that people engage randomly or whimsically. The church or the independent preacher should clearly announce the sermon posting time (especially for new online visitors) and, most importantly, post the sermon at exactly the agreed-upon time.

What

A sermon preached in the aphoristic script format works well, as Figure 9's sample shows. An aphoristic script sermon conveys several or many aphoristic (succinct) statements throughout its flow. This does not mean that the sermon will preach many loosely connected aphoristic claims (e.g., a multipoint sermon), each with emotionally or semantically powerful images attached. Rather, the sermon breaks down its main point into several subpoints, which are made clear through strong aphoristic claims.

One overarching thematic arc remains. The books of Proverbs or Ecclesiastes can help in understanding the aphoristic script format. Proverbs is not written in the narrative nor the prose style, but rather is full of insightful aphorisms connected closely to each other with an implicit yet recognizable overarching thematic flow. The Vidpod sermon is best poised for this kind of aphoristic proclamation for two reasons.

First, still or moving images, which are a significant part of the sermon message, constantly change. In many cases, those images *are* the subpoints of the sermon. Their inherent visual powers boost the semantic impact of the subpoints, almost in the sense of a one-to-one match. Naturally, prolonged narrative or prose writings cannot keep up with those fast-changing images with their distinct sermonic claims. Matching each aphoristic claim with each still or moving image is key to the effective seamless communication of the whole sermon.

Second, in the era of ChatGPT, what seems to be in demand is no longer needless wordiness or more information about life and the Bible (AI does this now in a second!), but interpersonal wisdom, unique insights from life experience, and words of real presence. ChatGPT or Wikipedia can't provide these, at least for now. Only real human voices embedded with genuine passion and compassion from trustworthy people achieve them. Aphorisms' condensed wording, which gets to the point even in one short sentence full of acute observation and analysis of human life, can be effective in maximizing the impact of the subpoints of the sermon.

Useful Homiletic Theory

What cannot go unnoticed in the practice of the Vidpod style is the preacher *being present while absent*. The preacher *is* present for sure, but with only through voice, which most conventional sermon viewers might see as the absence of the preacher's whole physio-personality. If this sounds like a grave issue, we would certainly need to consider it homiletically with more intensity. So, then, do we have any relevant homiletical discourse around the preacher being present while absent? In his insightful article in *Religions*, "Being There Even When You are Not: Presence in Distance Preaching," Tim Sensing seems to provide a clue to a possible resolution to the matter in focus, even though his argument is not focused on any variations of the Vidpod style.[4]

Building upon ideas of Terry A. Veling and Emmanuel Levinas, Sensing realizes that "preachers are often absent and not present even when preaching in the same room." In other words, there is always a chance that the preacher can be "other" to sermon listeners in the same space and time. Isn't it right that we human beings cannot really escape the inevitable existential condition of alienation or separation from each other, to borrow Paul Tillich's wisdom? Thus, for Sensing, in creating a firm sense of the presence of the preacher, it does not truly matter whether a preacher is actually there in person or on the digital screen. What does matter are the preacher's intentionality for presence and a twofold useful pastoral method that could achieve that purpose.

Citing the Epistle letters of Paul found in the New Testament and other ancient-rhetorical sources, Sensing proposes ethos as one of the finest pastoral methods for the preacher's intentional presence while being physically absent. He points out that Paul's letters were read among distant listeners while he was completely absent. Even so, the listeners received his words as if he had been there with them. How is this possible? It is because of the preacher Paul's pastoral ethos deeply embedded into his letters. Here pastoral ethos specifically means the preacher's credibility and authenticity. Put simply, when hearing messages via reading or recording from the absentee preacher, people ask, "Is this preacher trustworthy and genuinely caring for us?" If the answer is yes, listeners still recognize the preacher's presence among them and wholeheartedly accept the words spoken. This pastoral ethos, for Sensing, can be best achieved through the preacher's narrative identification with the listeners. In other words, through storytelling—sharing stories of daily life that the preacher and the listeners commonly experience (e.g., grocery incidents, movie watching, playing with children, driving to workplaces, and more)—the preacher is able to narrow the physical and psychological gaps between the preacher's own self and the listeners. Of course, Sensing acknowledges that the preacher's credibility and identification with the listeners will not develop overnight; this takes time. Thus, both the preacher and the listeners must be patient with each other and more intentional in establishing mutual trust in the digital space.

When applied to the Vidpod style specifically, the preacher will have to work hard to establish moral credibility and relational authenticity through modest self-disclosure and fine storytelling. Thankfully, relatable images and music—which Paul didn't have!—help a lot in this regard. When new sermon viewers start watching the Vidpod sermon, one of the very first questions in their mind is "Who on earth is this preacher? This preaching sounds amazing, but is this person trustworthy, is the message applicable, and does this person really care about me, even though we haven't met? (Plus, I don't see the preacher's countenance at all!)" If the sermon reviewers' answer is yes, the absentee Vidpod preacher's proclamation will be effective. What matters is the preacher's credibility and authenticity. More is discussed in Practical Tips below regarding simple yet efficient ways of increasing credibility and authenticity.

Practical Tips

- **Select Adoption of the Seven Traits: Shareability** is key to the sermonic communication of this style. The listeners or viewers have neither a church building nor a designated online space where they gather. They can be at any place, physically or virtually (e.g., YouTube, Instagram, Facebook, Twitter, Tumblr), where the prerecorded digital sermon is playable on any digital device. Easy access to the sermon content and its simple shareability on any online video platform are prerequisites for this style's effective communication.

  Ironically, without the preacher's bodily presence during the sermon, this style achieves (indeed, requires) a high level of **holistic artistry**. Music, acting, images, symbols, and various filming skills (e.g., close-up, time-lapse) all contribute to the artistry of the sermon. The trait of artistry has good potential to promote the **cross-cultural ubiquity** of the sermon. Thanks to the image-driven nature of the sermon, various images of the human race, culture, Jesus, and creation around the world can be easily incorporated into the sermon. Over a longer period of time, cross-cultural ubiquity may also be achieved by a series of sermons adopting various images of the written or incarnate Word. The possibilities for cross-cultural ubiquity are nearly unlimited.

- **Three, Five, Ten, or Fifteen Minutes:** The Vidpod sermon is highly flexible in terms of length. It could be a short three or five minutes, or a moderate length of ten or fifteen minutes. Generally, preachers do not produce Vidpod sermons running more than fifteen minutes due to people's short attention spans and video production difficulties. Briefer sermons work well as short midweek homilies or as trailers of longer Sunday morning sermons. Also, with three- or five-minute sermons, it is possible for the preacher to do a series of sermons having three to five episodes. These sermon series are great when the preacher wants to do verse-by-verse sermons with each episode exploring one verse at a time.

- **Free Images and Video Clips:** For those who are not familiar with digital images and video production, here is the good news. These days there are numerous free and subscription-based image and video clip providers online (e.g., unsplash.com and pixabay.com). Most laptops or desktop computers today have basic video editing tools. Thus, in a practical sense, there is no need for the preacher or the editing crew of the church to go outside, take photos and videos, and come back to the church office for countless hours of photoshopping and editing in order to align with the sermon content. (Remember that editing a simple fifteen-minute video can take hours!) No, the preacher can do it all in the home office, not even stepping outside for a second. What a world!

- **Plan Preaching Far Ahead:** Even when the preacher can do it all from an office, sermon writing and image/

video editing, combined altogether, will take a lot of time, not to mention the additional time involved if the preacher or the crew wants to do outside photography and video production. Thus, a wise preacher will plan sermons at least a month before their actual posting dates. Then the preacher will have time to write the sermon, begin collecting images and video clips, and also edit them along the way. Ideally, the preacher will have the entire year's sermons planned out at the beginning of the year, at least in terms of big ideas for each month or each sermon, so that whenever fine images or video clips happen to be in hand, the preacher can arrange them to match each sermon's key topic. Lectionary preachers having Scriptural passages already assigned for each Sunday may find this year-round process helpful.

- **Travel Wildly and Widely:** Yes, unlimited free images and video clips are available online. That said, the preacher's own photographs and video clips from the preacher's own trips would be highly valuable with great authenticity; for instance, during the sermon, the preacher can claim a spiritual or theological attachment to them. Thus, I encourage preachers to travel widely and wildly for richer and broader experiences of life and cultures around the nation and the world. Capture or videotape memorable moments and scenes, and upon coming back home, store them for later use with loosely connected thematic tags; you don't really know at the moment when and for what topic you'd want to use them, so loosely connected themes suffice.

- **An Online-Only Presence is Totally Okay:** As said above, an independent preacher—that is, with no physical building, denominational, or congregation connection—can practice the Vidpod style. All the preacher needs is a computer with an online connection. This situation raises all kinds of questions that could cause discomfort for most brick-and-mortar conventional churches and denominations; for instance, "Does this preacher have credentials like a proper ordination process, psychological screening, Association of Theological Schools–approved theological education, and no criminal background?" or "How does this preacher handle finances like offerings?" as well as "How can the preacher provide any pastoral services like visitation to the sick in the hospital?" The Vidpod style preacher may not be able to answer all of these and other relevant questions on a website or related online platforms (e.g., LinkedIn or YouTube channel). It is suggested, however, that the preacher provide as much information as possible to bolster credibility and accountability. For denominational preachers, providing their denominational affiliation would be great. Preachers are strongly encouraged to create their own website where the sermon viewers can interact with the preacher through live chat or sermon Q&A. (Free website/page-making programs are out there, such as Wix.com and WordPress.com.) The preacher's website will be the preacher's *real church*. So, make it a real congregational place with many other pastoral functions like pastoral prayers.

- **Friendly Hangout:** Whether you are an independent or congregational preacher, pastoral presence is still important in the practice of the Vidpod style. Independent preachers might consider occasional face-to-face online gatherings on Zoom or Google Meet. Meetings can be totally voluntary, with no strings attached. Ask people to bring their own coffee or meal and enjoy thirty minutes or an hour of communal time. Parish preachers may want to do this more structurally, with regular Friday noon coffee hour either in person or on Zoom.
- **No Retirement!:** This format may offer retired preachers the change for a second career as a pastoral service provider. Though small in numbers, these days there are some retired pastors posting their sermons on YouTube, Facebook, and other places. They do not minister to any particular church, but as John Wesley once said, they now have the entire world as their parish with which to share the good news of Christ. Those coming to and graduating from the seminary at a later stage of life who might not pursue a local congregational ministry could find the Vidpod style a fine option.

Final Remarks

In this era when AI-based voice interaction is possible between human beings and machines, the Vidpod style may face both positive receptions and pessimistic rejections. After all, Chat-GPT can even write a sermon on a particular biblical passage! People may eventually tire of hearing human voices alone through digital devices over and over again alongside other daily AI-based digital sounds and noises. On the other hand, however, the Vidpod style already might have become a friendly way of delivering the Christian message for the creative image- and meaningful sound-savoring people of today; for them, the preacher's appearance might not be essential for the gospel message. Why not? Didn't even God create the world in the Beginning through the Voice alone? Doesn't the writer of the Gospel say that in the Beginning there was the Word that is Jesus himself? He became human flesh, of course, like us at a certain point in history, but is his flesh not once more absent among us, coming to us again as the Word? Just like that, the Vidpod style may have strong theological backing.

Other Resources

E. M. Cioran, *The Trouble with Being Born* (New York: Arcade Publication, 2012).
   Readers will find the genius of Cioran's insightful aphorisms by simply reading through the volume and, hopefully, learn how to create their own.
Steven Ascher and Edward Pincus, *The Filmmaker's Handbook: A Comprehensive Guide for the Digital Age*, 5th ed. (New York: Plume, 2012).
   For a preacher who is new to (or even one familiar with) the Vidpod style, this will be an invaluable source, or a "film Bible," as people call it, thanks to its practical nuts-and-bolts guide to almost every aspect of filming.

Notes

1 In his recent Facebook feed, John S. McClure at Vanderbilt Divinity School calls this style the Vidpod sermon, a neologism created by

combining video and iPod. The communicative technique is almost the same with the Film style. The Vidpod sermon overlays the preacher's sermonic narration with a variety of relevant images and video clips. Like the Film style, the preacher does not necessarily show up in the sermonic Vidpod, except for the preacher's voice. A notable difference between the Film style and the Vidpod style is that the Film style tends to create a short sermonic film that has a coherent narrative structure, while the Vidpod style adopts disparate images and clips that can align with the sermon points. His sample sermon is available on YouTube:

"John McClure, Speak the Truth, VidPod Sermon, Oct 21, 2020, Vanderbilt Divinity School," November 18, 2020, accessed October 10, 2020, https://www.youtube.com/watch?v=2UHgVi86S7c&feature=youtu.be&fbclid=IwAR1vS1d710MUyqjrWvw1soLSpmw8UqwBtlM1lNwSDQWhPj4HIe8QQ0UG53s.

2 "Look To God For Courage (A Powerful Word Of Encouragement)," April 1, 2020, accessed October 10, 2020, https://www.youtube.com/watch?v=_09CDqhMCJI&feature=emb_title.

3 The term, naming grace, adapted from Hilkert, *Naming Grace: Preaching and the Sacramental Imagination*.

4 Tim Sensing, "Being There Even When You Are Not: Presence in Distance Preaching," *Religions* 14, no. 3 (March 6, 2023): 1—20, https://doi.org/10.3390/rel14030347.

CHAPTER 11

The Artist Style

Figure 10[1]

General Description

This style may more fully be described as the Arts and Biblical Talk style of preaching. The preacher will actually perform a piece of art in tandem with the sermon topic or content. For instance, when preaching on 2 Samuel 6:14-22 (David's Dance before the Ark), the preacher, if blessed with certain choreographic gifts (or if not, one can certainly dance before God without professional skills!), may present an imaginative performance of David's dance before, during, or after talking about the passage. Or when preaching on Romans 9:19-24 (God as the Potter and God's People as Clay), the preacher may want to sit around the (portable) pottery wheel and have an exegetical talk on the passage while actually spinning clay on the wheel.

The Drama style could be grouped as a subcategory under the Artist style, but I believe the two can be distinguished due to the Drama style's historical and continued popular use apart from other emerging forms of arts-based sermonic performances.

Details of the Style

Who

The preacher is the preaching artist. True, the Drama style and the Vidpod style also require the preacher's artistic sensibility and performance. The Artist style, however, distinguishes itself because the preacher actually performs during the sermon. Genres or forms of the arts that the preacher performs are practically unlimited: dancing, crafting, singing, filming, drawing, theatrical performing, poetic reading, designing, baking, dyeing, skiing, scuba diving, sculpting, modeling, photographing, and even walking. The preacher will perform an artistic piece inspired by the given passage or based on the given sermon message. This does not mean that the preacher should be a professional or a bi-vocational artist, though, of course, this may be the case for some preachers. The sermon viewers would not really expect that from the preacher. With a minor artistic sense and appreciation of the arts, however, any preacher can try the Artist style. After all, David before the Ark wasn't a professional dancer! When resources and time allow, preachers may want to learn about and practice different forms of the arts beyond their personal limits so that they can later make good use of them in Artist style preaching. Most important is exposure to various artistic works, performances, and events to keep the preacher's artistic sensibility fresh and updated. Preacher may find great joy in appreciating and practicing art genres that fit their homiletical interests.

Why

First and foremost, the Bible is full of art and artistic expressions. Think of how the book of Genesis begins and how the Book of Revelation unfolds. How about the Psalms, the Song of Songs, the parables of Jesus, the prophet Isaiah's heavenly vision, Mary's Song (the Magnificat), the Tabernacle design in Exodus, or King David's dance, among countless more examples throughout the Bible? Thus, the preacher as artist should not be a foreign concept. As the preaching artist, it is often the case that the preacher delivers multisensory messages that may convey all the logos (truth), ethos (goodness), and pathos (beauty) combined together as a genuine interpretation and proclamation of Scriptural passages.

The Artist style is good for online preaching because the online space itself can be highly aesthetic and artistic. Recall a typical Zoom screen, a YouTube page, or a church's web page where online preaching is streamed. We would easily recognize the aesthetic design of each page or screen, technically called industrial design. Thus, the Artist style, by which the preacher actually performs aesthetic biblical expressions (content), can align itself with its communicational medium (form) in great sync. In that sense, the Artist style could be an optimal choice.

It would be too presumptuous to say that the preacher can practice the Artist style on the entire Bible. There are surely many nonartistic accounts in historical or doctrinal writings like Leviticus or the Book of Romans. Hence, the Artist style would first be chosen for explicitly artistic passages. Even so, its style might be applicable to some historical or doctrinal writings. For instance, the preacher might draw the historical (or fictional) accounts surrounding the life of Queen Esther. Or how about singing about Paul's faith journey that led to his writing of Romans? In that regard, the opportunities of the Artist style can be limitless.

Where

The specific art form the preacher adopts might create minor restrictions regarding preaching places. Certainly, the preacher can perform many pieces of art before, during, or after the sermon in the church, that is, either at the pulpit or on the worship stage. Yet certain forms of art require different locations. For baking, the preacher might speak from the church's kitchen, and for photographing nature, the preacher could set up a station outside somewhere, like a nearby state park. Thanks to portable online live-streaming technology, preaching from these unconventional locations is totally possible. Occasionally, it would be simply wonderful to use actual art studios as preaching venues. For example, the preacher may want to make a visit to a local dancing studio, apparel shop, community theater, or ceramics studio.

When

Preaching can be either live streaming or prerecorded. For live streaming, the preacher should plan carefully on seamless integration of the artistic piece into the whole worship service and the verbal portion of the sermon. For instance, when a preacher, who typically preaches from the pulpit, wants to perform David's dance in the middle of a live-streaming sermon, the preacher has to move away from the pulpit to the stage area, perform there, and eventually come back to the pulpit. In all these moves, the camera should stream each action of the preacher smoothly while the preacher makes sure that there is no unnecessary interruption between the performance and the pulpit communication.

Again, the point is the full, seamless integration of art performance into the live sermon delivery; arts should not feel like inessential interruptions of the verbalized sermon.

The editing involved in prerecording could help minimize any interruptions between the artistic performance and the pulpit speech. Two options are available. First, the preacher may want to prerecord the artistic performance only and live stream the rest of the sermon. The preacher then will simply interpolate the prerecorded and edited performance into the sermon wherever it fits each time. Second, the entire sermon, including the performance, can be prerecorded, edited, and streamed. As one can easily imagine, a great benefit of prerecording is the liberty to choose the finest piece of several attempts of the same performance. Prerecording will surely lessen the burdens of an amateur artist by providing chances for several attempts and allowing after-performance editing.

What

The old saying, "two sides of the same coin" is the finest analogy for the intersectionality happening between verbal communication and performed art in this style. In other words, what the preacher speaks must enhance and illustrate what is performed, and vice versa. For that purpose, the artistic performance must be hermeneutical or interpretative; that is, performance as a critical interpretation of the given passage. The performance and any artistic artifacts that the preacher produces or brings as part of the sermon delivery must not be secondary props simply "attached" to the verbal communication, which can easily happen.

A great benefit of this total integration of the art performance into the making of the sermon is the holistic encounter of the Word of Christ. Sermon listeners or viewers today are eager not only to hear the sermon, but also to *see, taste, feel, and even touch* the compelling Word. That is, they are looking for more biblical-aesthetic or holistic-artistic multidimensional preaching, a type of preaching that can result in the multidimensional formation of one's self—both the preacher and the sermon viewers. As society becomes more visually oriented, art-seeking, and body-positive, the practice of preaching is likewise challenged to become more oriented toward the mind-body, word-visual, and artistic proclamation of the Sacred.

This holistic-aesthetic approach can be very helpful for any online preaching, as the sermon viewer's digital screen can be dry and spirit-less—two-dimensional space displaying a real person's three-dimensional preaching that happens somewhere else. An Artist style sermon, though still appearing in two dimensions, can add a good sense of embodiment, human connection, and aesthetic beauty to the verbal communication of the sermon. (After all, we still enjoy good movies on the digital screen!)

Intentionally aesthetic or artistic commentary is best in the Artist style. It would make little sense to develop a highly rationalistic or analytical verbalized segment when a performed art piece will be integrated with it. Sermon writing based on a holistic-artistic or performative-hermeneutical reading of Scripture is *a must* for this style.

In sum, the preacher's sermon preparation is twofold and thus literally doubles: the written and the performed. For this reason, the preacher may want to plan on a sermon at least a month or two weeks before actual delivery. This will allow ample time for the preacher and the worship crew to prepare necessary artistic elements, including securing appropriate performance venues and rehearsing the sermon and the target art piece.

Useful Homiletic Theory

A notable advantage of aesthetically-oriented preaching or the arts as a crucial performer of the Word is the experience of *mysterium tremendum et fansinans*—both *appalled and fascinated by God's Holy Mystery*—during the preaching event, to borrow Rudolf Otto's terminology. I have written elsewhere that the loss of the *mysterium* experience is one of the most fatal setbacks in modern homiletics and propose its recovery in the practice of preaching.[2] Two predominant homiletical methodologies in the local pulpit today—inductive and deductive—have made preaching either highly philosophical-conversational (inductive) or topical-didactic (deductive). Besides, both approaches tend to be quite cerebral-rationalistic and time-bound—that is, God's revelation happening (inductive) or becoming clear (deductive) only in the linear logical flow of time—even though inductive or so-called narrative preaching has tried to avoid that twofold pitfall. All these issues combined, I contend, have resulted in the significant loss of the *mysterium* experience in preaching; that is, the profound holistic religious encounter of the Word of Christ.

An essential kairos-oriented remedy for that problem is preaching being more aesthetic or the arts being a decisive performer of the Word. This suggestion can be explained in many different ways, but showing a concrete sample of its practical ramifications should suffice. The sample comes from Isaiah 6:

In the year that King Uzziah died, I saw the Lord sitting on a throne, high and lofty; and the hem of his robe filled the temple. Seraphs were in attendance above him; each had six wings: with two they covered their faces, and with two they covered their feet, and with two they flew. And one called to another and said:

"Holy, holy, holy is the Lord of hosts; the whole earth is full of his glory."

The pivots on the thresholds shook at the voices of those who called, and the house filled with smoke. And I said: "Woe is me! I am lost, for I am a man of unclean lips, and I live among a people of unclean lips; yet my eyes have seen the King, the Lord of hosts!" Then one of the seraphs flew to me, holding a live coal that had been taken from the altar with a pair of tongs. The seraph touched my mouth with it and said: "Now that this has touched your lips, your guilt has departed and your sin is blotted out." Then I heard the voice of the Lord saying, "Whom shall I send, and who will go for us?" And I said, "Here am I; send me!" (Isa 6:1–8, NRSV)

As seen in the above passage, which describes how Isaiah is born as a prophet and preacher, an aesthetical-holistic homiletical event—a Word event—occurs to Isaiah in the threefold way that leads to his tremendous *mysterium* encounter. First off, this Word event is obviously kairos-oriented; Isaiah is led into the heavenly vision where time is eternal and every single moment is revelatory of God's Glory. There, second, Isaiah gets the fully embodied experience of the Divine; to see, smell, feel, and even touch, beyond auditory experience alone. Last, he is both so *mysterium*-appalled and fascinated by the Divine's presence and prophetic call that he blurts out, "Here am I; send me!" What a mystery, and what a holistic-aesthetic Word event! A faithful servant of God is born out of that experience.

The Artist style of online preaching has great potential to accomplish all these *mysterium*-oriented homiletical merits, thanks to its highly aesthetic-holistic, fully bodily nature. Admittedly, there are experiential limits on the side of the sermon viewers, who must watch the preacher's or the artist's sermonic performance on the two-dimensional flat screen. As mentioned before, however, people are today accustomed to thoroughly enjoying 3D performance on the 2D digital screen. In the same way, the Artist style will draw sermon viewers into the aesthetic-holistic, *mysterium* encounter of the Divine.

Practical Tips

- **Select Adoption of the Seven Traits:** No doubt, **Holistic artistry** is at the core of the sermon's making and delivery. The preacher reads Scripture through a multisensory interpretive lens or, better, encounters holistic-artistically the Divine's working in it, which will all be communicated aesthetically later in verbal speech and art performance. The intellectual or spiritual impact of holistic artistry on the episteme and heart of the sermon viewer can be enhanced by well-maneuvered camera movements, like zoom in and zoom out. For instance, when the preacher does a theatrical performance, the camera would zoom in on the face of the preacher so that the sermon viewers can see delicate emotional changes expressed in the face. Or, when preaching is prerecorded outside in nature, the camera may want to show a panoramic view of the specific natural location in the middle of which preaching happens as if preaching was part of the natural world.

Cross-Cultural Ubiquity: Cross-cultural ubiquity can also be a strong homiletical trait of the Artist style. When possible, the preacher, though limited by cultural context and experiences, may want to integrate unfamiliar artistic expressions of faith from many different cultures into the aesthetic delivery of the sermon. For instance, when showing cinematic expressions of Christian faith around the world, the preacher may want to display different cultural portraits of Jesus: Jesus as Korean, Indian, Chinese, African, Middle Eastern, Latino, American, and so on. When having a conversation on the Lord's Table, the preacher may want to show how different elements can be used as "bread" and "wine" such as rice cake and pure water where there is no bread and wine available.

- **Time Allocation:** Should the words spoken or the art performed get more time? Before answering the question, one should consider several variations available for the Artist style: 1) verbal-art-verbal, 2) art-verbal-art, 3) verbal-art, 4) art-verbal, and 5) synchronization of verbal and art (e.g., paint while talking throughout), and potentially others. In the case of verbal-art-verbal, there is a good chance that talking would get more time, while the opposite could happen in the practice of art-verbal-art. An even overall split might be ideal in most cases. At times, however, the ratio could be 3:7 (talking:performing) or 6:4 (talking:performing). Beware of leaning too far in one direction; 1:9 or 9:1 would not be a fine allocation at all.

- **Rehearsal, Rehearsal:** The importance of rehearsal can't be overemphasized. The complexity of liturgical logistics involving the whole worship and an artistic performance alongside the speech portion requires highly detailed planning. Even for prerecording, rehearsal is essential to reduce the need for on-site impromptu planning and performative errors. Ideally the whole sermon script and a relevant artistic piece are ready at least two weeks before the actual delivery, and the rehearsal happens at least a couple of times, including in the actual sermon delivery space. If available, rehearsals should be recorded for the review of the preacher and worship crew.

- **Take Art Lessons:** Surely, the preacher does not have to be an art professional in any specific art area in any sense. But if a preacher has some artistic gift(s), why not further hone them? Options could be available around town at a YMCA, local dance studio, music studio, ceramics academy, ethnic cultural center (e.g., Japanese language and culture center), and the like. Many artists also provide prerecorded free lessons on YouTube, and affordable paid art lesson plans are also available online, either synchronous or asynchronous. Trying any of these options could be quite refreshing and meaningful as continued pastoral development opportunities.

- **Collaboration with an Artist:** There is one fine "solution" for preachers who think they may not have any artistic gifts but still wants to try the Artist style: collaboration with the artists in their own congregation or town. This can happen at least in three ways: 1) the artist's performance and the preacher's speech (see variations available above in Time Allocation), 2) the artist's performance and then the preacher's pastoral interview-style talk with the artist as a conversational sermon, and 3) the preacher's speech and artistic collaboration with the artist (the preacher will join the artist in the art performance with the artist's guide). In adopting any of these collaborative sermon types, collective study of Scripture by the pastor and the artist is important. They will need to have enough holistic-artistic, interpretive conversations along the way on the sermon passage that their art performance and speech appear in fine sync, fully supporting and illustrating the other. A fine balance and close intersection between the two must always be sought.

Final Remarks

Thus far, we've dealt only with the practical aspect of an artistic performance or the arts in general: what to do, and how to do it. Yet before concluding the chapter, we'd better recall that any artistic performance is a philosophical activity too. That is, behind or beneath the practicality of the arts, there is always a philosophical underpinning (e.g., cubist-philosophical reasoning beneath cubist paint). Some basic familiarity with artistic-philosophical streams will surely help the Artist preacher better understand and practice each different artistic form in preaching.

For that purpose, two suggestions will suffice. First, read thoroughly at least one brief art history book. (See a book suggestion below.) Second, conduct a Google image search for each artistic philosophy or use any other search engines for the same purpose, and pay attention to those images—painting, dancing, architecture, installation, fashion, sculpture, crafts, and so forth. Film or music searches on YouTube may also be helpful. All these certainly help preachers, especially when they want to collaborate closely with artists, as suggested in Practical Tips.

Other Resources

Sunggu A. Yang, *Arts and Preaching: An Aesthetic Homiletic for the Twenty-First Century* (Eugene, OR: Cascade Books, 2021).
This volume showcases several samples of doing light theological exploration of the author-chosen art forms, among other merits.
Marilyn Stokstad and Michael Watt Cothren, *Art: A Brief History*, 6th ed. (Boston: Pearson, 2015).
The volume covers various art forms and artistic movements, from the ancient time to the modern, and around the globe. The preacher may want to give keen attention to modern art movements as they are highly relevant to the people today.

Notes

1 "Mark Anthony Preaching and Painting in Our Church.," July 7, 2013, accessed March 1, 2023,https://www.youtube.com/watch?v=WfpNwsWty2k.

2 Sunggu Yang, "Homiletical Aesthetics: A Paradigmatic Proposal for a Holistic Experience of Preaching," *Theology Today* 73, no. 4 (2017): 364–77, https://doi.org/10.1177/0040573616669563.

EPILOGUE

Online preaching—a moment of déjà vu, yet realistic.

Between December 2022 and February 2023, the whole world thought that it could move on to being in person again, and the churches reopened their doors; we all thought online preaching was no longer in demand. Then severe winter storms in many parts of the nation proved that notion wrong. Portland, Oregon, where I currently reside, experienced a lot of snow and dangerous icy roads, and churches had to close their doors again. Church services went online, rekindling the demand for online preaching. It was temporary this time, only with a couple of Sundays online. But it made a clear point that online preaching is now a norm for the church—it's no longer a stranger!—and there will be occasions for online preaching moving forward.

The icy storms created one special occasion for online preaching. Yet, the truth is that online preaching has become and will become a stable part of the church's life. As I write this epilogue, I realize that the COVID pandemic has been addressed in ways that allow most, if not all, worshippers to return to their church pews and preachers to their pulpits. However, given that new viruses and hybrid versions of COVID may still threaten us, it is entirely possible that preachers will need to continue developing their online ministries of preaching the Word digitalized.[1] Furthermore, in today's world, it is unlikely that many congregations will meet exclusively in person and very likely that they will be utilizing online platforms for worship and preaching in the foreseeable future. For all those cases and more, this volume is intended to help preachers to consider the options for *the Word digitalized*, including the opportunities and challenges that different styles invite. At the very least, we should continue to develop homiletical tools that are communicatively effective and theologically sound for the digital, online era. Even in times of nonpandemic crisis, we can further diversify our modes and styles of preaching to fit situations that favor an online approach (e.g., providing a message of hope for those who are isolated or may find a worship community online while living in remote places or experiencing natural catastrophes). Whatever our circumstances may be, learning and further developing a theology of online preaching and its types, along with accompanying digital skills, is of great importance for preachers today—both seasoned and emerging ones. We hope to see more educational, theological, and critical resources related to online preaching in the near future.

Finally, preachers practicing online preaching must continue to study social and online communicative dynamics. Digital platforms of communication and message content change constantly, faster than we may even notice. This means that there is a good chance that other types of online preaching beyond the ten listed above may emerge sooner rather than later. Preachers will want to seize, rather than chase after, the pace, moving ahead in creating their own operative online preaching theory and practice.

Notes

1 In 2018, the CDC (Centers for Disease Control and Prevention) already predicted that different kinds of pandemics could happen again in the future. The coronavirus of 2020 is only one of them. See the CDC's article, "The 1918 Flu Pandemic: Why It Matters 100 Years Later," on its website:

"The 1918 Flu Pandemic: Why It Matters 100 Years Later," *Public Health Matters* (blog), May 14, 2018, accessed October 10, 2020, https://blogs.cdc.gov/publichealthmatters/2018/05/1918-flu/.

Also, see CNN's "Hunting for 'Disease X,'" https://www.cnn.com/2020/12/22/africa/drc-forest-new-virus-intl/index.html (accessed on December 22, 2020).

Working Preacher BOOKS

Good Preaching
Changes Lives

Working Preacher Books is a partnership between Luther Seminary, WorkingPreacher.org, and Fortress Press.

Books in the Series

Real People, Real Faith: Preaching Biblical Characters by Cindy Halvorson

The Visual Preacher: Proclaiming an Embodied Word by Steve Thomason

Divine Laughter: Preaching and the Serious Business of Humor by Karl N. Jacobson and Rolf A. Jacobson

For Every Matter under Heaven: Preaching on Special Occasions by Beverly Zink-Sawyer and Donna Giver-Johnston

Preaching the Gospel of Justice: Good News in Community by Jennifer L. Ackerman

Digital Homiletics: The Theology and Practice of Online Preaching by Sunggu A. Yang